UNLOCK YOUR MIND

To Torben and Torsten

UNLOCK YOUR MIND

A practical guide to deliberate and systematic innovation

Dennis Sherwood

Gower

Published by
Gower Publishing Limited
Gower House
Croft Road
Aldershot
Hampshire GU11 3HR
England

Gower
Old Post Road
Brookfield
Vermont 05036
USA

Dennis Sherwood has asserted his right under the Copyright, Designs and Patents Act 1988 to be identified as the author of this work.

British Library Cataloguing in Publication Data
Sherwood, Dennis, 1949–
   Unlock your mind : a practical guide to deliberate and systematic innovation
   1. Creative ability in business   2. Organizational change
   I. Title
   658.4'063

   ISBN 0 566 07983 6

Library of Congress Cataloguing-in-Publication Data
Sherwood, Dennis, 1949–
   Unlock your mind : a practical guide to deliberate and systematic innovation /
   Dennis Sherwood
      p. cm.
   Includes bibliographical references and index.
   ISBN 0–566–07983–6 (hardback)
   1. Technological innovations—Management.   2. Inventions.
   I. Title
   HD45.S42 1988   97–28138
   658.5'77—dc21   CIP

Typeset in Plantin Light by Photoprint, Torquay, Devon, and printed in Great Britain by MPG Books, Bodmin.

CONTENTS

LIST OF FIGURES

FOREWORD

I first met Dennis Sherwood when he was hosting a corporate event at which I was to be a speaker, but our early conversations were mostly about music. To my astonishment, I discovered this 'businessman' was not only knowledgeable about classical music, but deeply responsive to the subtle nuances of music's passionate voice. Since then we have discovered a shared fascination for the creative process itself and a belief that this capacity for innovation is an essential ingredient of all successful entreprises. Innovation is, in essence, the ability to think, to distinguish one thing from another. Without it we are condemned to replay the record of habit over and over; he who embraces and masters it, however, has the key to 'leap the fences' to effectiveness, expressivity and joy.

As a musician and conductor, I take as a given the belief that great music is for everyone. Music's capacity to allow each sound to soar, as it were, on the wings of song, is ours by birthright. And yet we know, all too well, how easily discouragement, a negative attitude and non-use condemns so many to incomprehension and non-participation. But all that was ever needed was a great teacher who could guide us to unlock the mysteries and crack the musical code.

Innovation, the subject of this book, is equally a capacity given to all humans beings. But disuse and the fear of making a mistake prevents access for most of us, especially in times of stress, when it becomes almost essential. Again, all that is required is a great teacher to point the way and remind us of the pitfalls – the entrenched paths that, like those caused by rain in a valley over a period of thousands of years, keep us locked in a prison of habit. Dennis Sherwood is just such a teacher. With infinite care and lightness of touch, he takes the reader into the mysteries of innovation and reveals how great teamwork can unleash creativity within us all. He is a gentle provocateur, who invites us, through humour, anecdote, example and analysis to question our assumptions and completely re-evaluate our organizational thinking.

Benjamin Zander
Boston Philharmonic

PREFACE

Greetings, gentle reader,
                              Here is something pretty neat:
It's a formal introduction to a boogie-woogie beat.
If the rhythm really gets you, you may want to stomp your feet
Or to clap your hands and rock from side to side within your
    seat.

Well, my subject's innovation – how to foster ideas new;
It's important for ourselves and for our org'nizations too.
Is it simply inspiration? Lightning striking from the blue?
Or is there science? Is there process? Are there things that you
    can do?

Perhaps the answer's simple: just hire Newton, Einstein, Planck,
Any bunch of friendly gurus to create your own think-tank.
But the problem's the supply side – you will surely draw a blank
On recruitment: there just aren't enough good people of first
    rank.

Another way, perhaps, might be to copy, cheat, or steal
Someone else's bright ideas – why should you reinvent the wheel?
To steal, though, sounds despicable; to benchmark's more genteel.
The issue here is secrecy – how much would you reveal?

To me, the answer's different, for to nurture innovation
You must find a way to motivate, provoke the liberation
Of the power of the people in the whole organization:
That means you, and me, and us – we all have great imagination!

Fine words, for sure. But are they true? Have I just set a trap?
Do we have the tools, techniques? A process? Methods and a
    map?
We do! Your job you can inject with flair, pizzazz and zap!
And to tell you how, it's back to prose, so now I'll end my rap!

That's that!

Well, if you're going to write a book on innovation, you may as well start
in an innovative way!

Yes, I know it's a silly rhyme; but it does encapsulate many of the major themes of this book: is innovation just a question of luck, of lightning happening to strike in the right place at the right time? Or do you have to be 'a creative person', with the IQ of a genius and the temperament of a great artist? Or is it more a matter of keeping your eyes open and copying someone else's ideas?

The answer to all of these questions is a resounding 'no', for the two key messages of this book are:

- **The ability to innovate is in us all.**
- **The process of innovation can be deliberate, systematic and safe.**

These messages are enormously powerful, and empowering, for everyone can contribute. And the purpose of this book is to explain how.

Part 1, 'Patterns', explains just what innovation is, and what it is not. Here you will discover that innovation is not about some supreme creative act in which something is created out of nothing; rather, innovation is about forming a new pattern of pre-existing components.

Part 2, 'Ideas', shows you how to innovate in business, where the 'components' are the experience and knowledge of yourself and your colleagues, and the new 'pattern' you are seeking is the generation of a new idea to design a new product, or a new process, or to solve a particular problem. This, the heart of the book, covers:

- how to generate new ideas
- where to look for new ideas
- some tools and techniques to make the process of innovation focused, deliberate and systematic
- how to evaluate ideas in a balanced manner.

Part 3, 'Teamwork', is based on the recognition that, although you can innovate by yourself, the process of innovation is far richer, and much more likely to give better results, when carried out in high-performing teams. This takes us into the territory of interpersonal behaviours, organizational cultures and personal and organizational learning, with excursions into such high-performing teams as Nelson's navy and the symphony orchestra. Given the nature of the material, don't be surprised if you find this part of the book quite demanding!

Dennis Sherwood

ACKNOWLEDGEMENTS

As I have already noted, innovation is not about creating something out of nothing, and this book is no exception. Numerous books have been written on innovation and creativity and, in writing this one, I have of course drawn heavily on existing works. May I therefore acknowledge my indebtedness to Arthur Koestler whose work, *The Act of Creation*, although published over 30 years ago, is a veritable goldmine of wisdom; to Edward de Bono, whose library of over 40 books contains many profound insights; and to Peter Senge, author of *The Fifth Discipline*, whose ideas have greatly influenced Part 3. I also thank Roger von Oech for granting permission for me to use some selections from his *Creative Whack Pack* to enliven my narrative.

May I also take this opportunity to thank the very many friends, colleagues and participants at my seminars and workshops who have all, directly or indirectly, contributed. In particular, may I mention Rob Eastaway, Benjamin Zander, Alison Bott, Tarn Phillips, Penny Hembrow, Amanda Harvey, Khaled Choudhury, André-Benôit de Jaegère and Yendi Dial; Richard Gibbon of the National Railway Museum at York; Jackie Cottrell and Sultan Kermally of the Economist Conferences, as well as Julia Scott and Solveig Gardner Servian at Gower. And thanks, of course, also to Anny, Torben and Torsten who had to cope with a highly task-oriented husband and father.

DS

PART *1*

PATTERNS

The creative act is not an act of creation in the sense of the Old Testament. It does not create something out of nothing; it uncovers, selects, re-shuffles, combines, synthesises already existing facts, ideas, faculties, skills. The more familiar the parts, the more striking the new whole.

(Arthur Koestler, *The Act of Creation*)

1 WHAT IS INNOVATION?

What this book is about

As this book is about ideas and how to get them, I am using the term 'innovation' to refer to the process by which new ideas are generated and realized. And by 'new', I mean anything that is new to you or your organization – anything that is different, even only modestly so, from what has gone before. This definition encompasses not only new concepts in products or services, but also new processes and systems, and new ways of interacting with people. So my use of the term 'innovation' is broad and general and is not restricted to 'new product development' or 'how to get things to market'.

My definition of innovation does, I am sure, agree with what many of us would regard as common sense, and it also demystifies what is sometimes regarded as an almost magical concept. To me, innovation is not about having a completely original 'unique' thought; it does not require an act of superhuman genius. But it does require a different attitude to thinking, as well as the self-confidence to explore what must be – by definition – uncharted territory: clearly, if your objective is to find something new, something different, you must look in a different place, or perhaps look in familiar places in a rather different way. Or, as Roger von Oech puts it in his *Creative Whack Pack*, if the good idea you need is behind you, you won't find it by looking twice as hard at what's in front.

So, my purpose is twofold. First, it is to demonstrate utterly convincingly that all of us have the power and capacity to innovate, provided that three conditions hold:

- **We must have the self-confidence that, yes, we can do it.**
- **We must be familiar with a few tools and techniques to help us think in perhaps unfamiliar ways.**
- **And, if we are part of an organization, we must recognize that our organization's culture, and our styles of interpersonal behaviour, can have a profound influence on innovation, from energizing and facilitating it, to killing it stone dead.**

Second, it is to guide you as to what you, both as an individual and as a contributor to a larger organization, can do to make innovation happen.

Why bother?

But why should you bother? Why can't you just leave innovation to someone else?

Well, you can.

If you want to, that is. If you believe that tomorrow, and the next day, and the next will all be the same as yesterday, the day before and the day before that, then you can indeed continue to behave in exactly the same way as you always have. For you have no reason to wish to do anything differently.

But if you do not wish to behave as a preprogrammed robot, if you do wish not only to react to external changes and stimuli as they happen but also to anticipate them and influence them, then innovation is important. Crucially so. Innovation is also good business, as that most innovative company, 3M, knows all too well . . .

CASE FILE

Why bother?

One of the most consistently innovative companies in the world is the engineering company, 3M, famous for industrial abrasives, magnetic tapes and the 'yellow sticky' – the ubiquitous Post-it® notes. 3M is so committed to innovation that it has two corporate goals directly linked to innovation: 10 per cent of annual sales are targeted to come from products that have been in the market for just one year, and 30 per cent from products introduced over the previous four years.

Why do they bother?

In the 1996 'UK Innovation Lecture', Dr William Coyne, 3M's senior Vice-President for Research and Development gave a disarmingly simple answer:

Innovation is the key to growth because it delights our customers. That delight is the basis for long-lasting customer loyalty.

One of the great spurs to innovation has been the business fad of the '90s – process re-engineering. The goal of business process re-engineering has been variously defined as 'to achieve a step change, quantum leap, in performance', 'to do new things' or 'to do existing things substantially differently'. All the textbooks then describe the process of re-engineering as a series of steps, usually involving:

- benchmarking your own performance against a competitor, or some form of analogue, so as to create an incentive to change, or to define a goal to strive for
- analysing your existing processes so as to provide good data concerning 'here'
- creating an environment whereby people accept the changes necessary to move from 'here' to 'there'.

The fundamental problem of re-engineering, however, is to define just where 'there' is. If the goal is to do existing things substantially differently, or to do new things altogether, how do you generate the new ideas in the first place? You can analyse existing processes until you are blue in the face, and you will certainly identify a whole host of things that can be improved to some degree. But is this a quantum leap?

Suppose, for example, that you had been asked to re-engineer a computer keyboard. You would have analysed in great detail how keystrokes are made, and how different clusters of letters are statistically distributed in any given language. As a result, you would probably come up with some very sensible ideas on how to redesign the keyboard; with the keys in different places, and perhaps of different sizes. Oh yes, people will have to be retrained to 'unlearn' the typing skills acquired by years of experience using a conventional QWERTY keyboard (designed, of course, specifically to avoid the glueing together of those mechanical arms they used to have for each letter on pre-electronic typewriters), but that's what change management is all about, isn't it?

But would you have come up with the idea of a 'mouse'?

Yes, you can prepare people for change; but to what purpose if the change is only marginal? To a certain extent, external benchmarking can suggest alternatives which you may be able to copy, but to rely solely on benchmarking must surely be inadequate. If you are a follower, the best you will be able to achieve is to ape the leader, who, by the time you have achieved the target performance, will have moved on anyway. And if you are the leader, against whom do you benchmark? 'Against an organization in a different industry,' I hear you say. Yes, that's true too. But what stops an organization striving to do better, to foster new ideas, to transcend its own current levels of performance, of its own accord? For that, to me, is where true leadership lies – in that inner drive to excel, in that positive dissatisfaction, in that constructive restlessness that the status quo is never good enough. As we shall see, benchmarking does indeed have a role to play, but only as a contributor to the much larger picture – that of true innovation.

What does innovation look and feel like?

PAUSE FOR THOUGHT

Imagine that you are visiting an organization which is famous for its creativity and innovation.

What would you see? Hear? Experience?

How does this differ from what you would experience if you were visiting an organization famed for its *lack* of innovation and creativity?

Most people, when asked to describe the 'look and feel' of an innovative organization, use words such as:

Lively	Young	No manuals
Open	White-boards	Delegation
Noisy	Pictures	Teams
Laughter	Excitement	Flexibility
Flat-structured	Variety of dress	Respect
Yes! Yes! Yes!	More women than men	Trust
Lots of light	Flexitime	Sharing
Plenty of space	Payment by results	Success
Lots of personal touches	Lots of waste-paper baskets	Lots of books, magazines
A communal area where people can chat	People treated as individuals to be developed	Lots of contact with the world outside

Individuals, not clones	Fun	Happy
Energy	Learning	Serendipity rules OK!
Healthily sceptical	Provocative	Supportive
Decisive leadership	Willing followership	Teams, not individuals
Friendly	Enthusiastic	Entrepreneurial
Listening	Questioning	Exploring
Risk-taking	Knowledge is seen as a shared resource	Informal
Untidy	Lots of computers	Training
No offices	Few rules	Colour

In contrast, the descriptions of uninnovative organizations usually read like this:

Sterile	Little natural light	Lots of rules
Hierarchy	Long corridors	Precedent rules OK!
Old	Politics	More men than women
Silent	Safe, if you conform	White shirts
Lots of walls	Training at a minimum	Efficient
People treated as costs to be controlled	Lots of paper, but almost neurotically tidy	Procedures, procedures, procedures
Clones, not individuals	Fear	Hard-working
Payment by toeing the line	Knowledge seen as a source of internal competitive advantage	Mistakes to be avoided at all costs
Boring	Old-fashioned	No! No! No!
Where's the business case?	Nothing ever questioned	Junior staff 'know their place'
Risk averse	Slow	Secretive
Impersonal	Dull	Telling, not asking
Humourless	9 to 5	Regimented
Minimum contact with the outside world	Individual success takes priority over teams	We tried that once – it didn't work
We know it all	Advocacy, not debate	Uniform
Emotions not allowed	Logic, not intuition	Defensive
Don't argue with the boss	I'm right, you're wrong	Seniority wins over merit
Judgemental	Highly status conscious	Narrow
Quick to evaluate	Answers, not questions	Complacent
Closed	Talking, not listening	Bureaucratic

Compare your thoughts with those shown on the preceding pages: these descriptions, by the way, are not just my words, but are drawn from the flipcharts compiled during the many workshops I have run with clients.

There will, of course, be many differences in detail, but I suspect there is considerable harmony between your views on what an innovative environment looks and feels like – and indeed an uninnovative environment – and the sentiments expressed during my workshops. Of course, there is an inevitable element of stereotyping and fantasy, with the innovative environment seeming like an ideal 60s hippy paradise, and the uninnovative one vying with an adult version of Dotheboys Hall for mean-mindedness; but within the exaggeration, is there not more than a gleam of truth?

To me, the two most salient features of the lists are these:

- Neither list makes any reference to the presence, or absence, of individuals with particular academic, intellectual or artistic talents. Indeed, on no occasion have I ever seen any group write, on the 'innovative' side, items such as 'full of Einsteins, Michelangelos, and Mozarts', or, on the 'uninnovative' side, 'no Einsteins, Michelangelos or Mozarts'.
- Almost every item on both lists refers to some aspect of organization, or interpersonal behaviour, or culture.

Yes, you too can do it

What is the take-home lesson from this?

Surely it is an innate recognition that innovation is not about being Einstein, Michelangelo or Mozart; rather, innovation is very much about the way in which we relate to one another, and the environment we create around ourselves.

This is a profoundly positive message.

If we wish to be innovative, we *all* have the opportunity to create around ourselves the kind of environment which maps onto the first list, rather than the second. Even if your organization is less rather than more receptive to new ideas, what stops you from creating your own microenvironment in your own department?

Let me cite some examples.

Imagine you are holding a meeting to explore a particular issue – say, how best to launch a new product. As the departmental manager, the senior person, you are chairing the meeting. What kind of atmosphere do you create? Do you encourage everyone to participate, or do you dominate? Do you listen to other people's ideas, or do you show visible signs of irritation whenever someone else is in the limelight? Do junior people feel able to express themselves, or are they browbeaten by the more senior people? And which of these styles promotes innovation, and which stifles it?

Of course, your meetings are models of best practice. But perhaps you have sat in meetings chaired by others that weren't quite so cosy.

A second example. For several weeks, you have been wrestling with a particular problem. Suddenly, you have a great idea. Full of excitement, you go to your boss to explain it. Your boss's immediate response is to identify all the reasons why your idea won't work. And when that highly enjoyable game has run its course, your boss then probes every nook and cranny of your thinking to expose the logical flaws. How do you feel after that? And what encouragement is that for you to come up with further 'good ideas'? Far, far better to play safe.

Innovation, then, is very much a creation of the environment – an environment which is under your control. So, control – or better, empower – it. What stops you from making the environment around you a nursery of innovation?

This does not imply, of course, that we should all spend all our time coming up with new ideas; nor does it imply that all ideas, by definition, are good ones.

As with all other aspects of life, innovation has its time and place. Yes, of course I am an advocate of deliberate innovation, but that does not distort my recognizing that, in many circumstances, the tried, tested, dull, boring routine is exactly appropriate. I am indeed quite glad that, when I'm in an aeroplane, the pilot chooses to follow standard procedures when landing and doesn't decide to try a new idea to see what happens, for example, if we land backwards. But the pilot might have some very good ideas for improving, say, the visibility of cockpit instrumentation, and should be allowed the space to express them.

Nor should it be assumed that all ideas are necessarily 'good' and commercially viable. Many ideas are quite loony, but we will never know unless they are articulated and explored. And, as we shall see, the exploration of an apparently 'nutty' idea might lead to a singularly sensible one. What we need is a sense of safety in articulating what might be perceived as a crazy idea, a fair process for exploring the idea, and a commercially rational manner of deciding between the good and the bad: needs that will all be satisfied as you read further into this book.

So, to summarise:

● The capacity to innovate is in us all.
● The process of innovation is very sensitive to the cultures of our organizations and our styles of interpersonal behaviour. This is good news. We can all decide how we personally wish to behave, and we can all at least try to influence our organizations.
● Innovation should not be an overarching objective for its own sake. For much of our time – perhaps most of it – it is quite appropriate to follow the tried and tested routes. But wouldn't it be good to be able to press the innovation button when we want to and need to?
● There is no law saying that all ideas are good ones. Many of them aren't. So we need a safe way of separating the wheat from the chaff. A way that is commercially rational, that doesn't hurt (too much) and – most importantly – that does not act as a positive disincentive for anyone ever to dare to open their mouths again.

2 BEETHOVEN AND THE BEATLES

Where does innovation come from?

Where would you look for the best examples of innovation? When I ask this question in my workshops, the most frequent responses are:

- **an artist's studio**
- **an advertising agency**
- **a jam session of a pop group**
- **a design consultancy.**

We can all understand why these environments are associated with innovation and creativity, but, to identify the true basis of innovation, we need to look deeper, and in another direction.

Let me take you on a journey . . .

Music

PAUSE FOR THOUGHT

What are the key differences between Beethoven and the Beatles?

I expect your list contains such items as:

- Beethoven was German; the Beatles came from Liverpool.
- Beethoven wrote classical music; the Beatles wrote pop.
- Beethoven wrote music for many different types of ensemble, from the orchestra to the solo piano; the Beatles wrote primarily for their own group.
- Beethoven composed around the 1800s, the Beatles composed around the 1960s.

And had the question been to identify the key similarities, your response might have been:

- Both used music as a medium for expression.
- Both used music based on normal Western major and minor 12 note scales.
- Both had long hair.
- Both were regarded by their contemporaries as mildly outrageous.
- Both were great innovators: Beethoven was the first composer to merge the movements of a concerto (the last two movements of the 'Emperor' Piano Concerto); the Beatles were the first to create a theme album in which the songs merged into one another (*Sergeant Pepper's Lonely Hearts Club Band*).
- They were both very creative. In fact, there is a (totally spurious!) argument that the Beatles were more creative: Beethoven's 'theme tune', the opening bars of the *Fifth Symphony* comprises eight notes of which four are different (see Figure 2.1); the theme tune of the Beatles' *She Loves You*, covers four different notes in a sequence of just six (Figure 2.2).

The list of similarities is alarmingly long. What, then, *is* the difference?

Figure 2.1   The opening notes of Beethoven's *Fifth Symphony*

Figure 2.2   The opening notes of the Beatles' *She Loves You*

It must have something to do with music, but they both used the same musical source – the notes to be found on a standard piano. Perhaps a clue can be found by considering what would happen if you tried to identify the composer of just a single note. If you heard any single note – middle C or whatever – just by itself, it would be impossible to determine who 'composed' it: the answer can only be no-one or everyone. But if you heard the familiar 'bo-bo-bo boom, bo-bo-bo boom', you would immediately recognise Beethoven's *Fifth*.

The answer cannot lie in the characteristics of a single note, but must be something to do with the characteristics of groups of notes. What, though, is the difference between a single note and a group? There can be only one answer: whereas a single note is isolated, a group of notes forms a sequence, a pattern. Yes, that's it. It's all about sequences, patterns. The difference between Beethoven's *Fifth Symphony* and *She Loves You* is simply that they are different patterns of the same basic component parts!

Wait a moment, though. Isn't that true of all music? Yes. Well, nearly all music, at least in the Western tradition.

Almost all Western music simply consists of different patterns of a selection of notes drawn from a common master set. And the master set is not that big: a standard modern piano has just 88 notes, but in practice, those at the extreme upper and lower ends of the range are rarely used – most music can be played on the central four octaves spanning just 48 different notes.

So, innovation in music, as represented by the differences between Beethoven and the Beatles, Gounod and Gershwin, and Liszt and Lloyd-Webber, is determined not by the 'invention' of new notes, but by combining *existing* notes in new, different *patterns*, each expressing its own unique musical idea.

Is this a clue to the true basis of innovation? Perhaps . . .

Literature

A second source of marvellous innovation is literature: every new book is an example of new ideas and new thoughts. And just as we enquired into the fundamental differences between Beethoven and the Beatles, we can ask the same question of Shakespeare and Steinbeck. Both wrote great literature, and both wrote in the English language. And, for the most part, they expressed their thoughts by drawing from the same master set of component parts – the words of the English language. Yes, there are some differences in vocabulary, but this is primarily attributable to differences in usage between sixteenth-century England and twentieth-century North America. In essence, the difference between Shakespeare and Steinbeck lies in the differences in the patterns formed by the same words. Occasionally, a Joyce or a Lear coins a new word but, for the most part, the incredibly rich variety of literature in the English language is a matter of patterns. As with innovation in music, which arises from different patterns of the same notes, innovation in literature is principally a process of forming new patterns from existing words, in order to reflect new thoughts. The same concept, of course, applies to literature in other languages.

But, in literature, we can discern a yet deeper level of innovation – of patterns. If we look beyond the literature to the words themselves, all of the many thousands of different words in the lexicon of the English language are formed by different patterns of just 26 different components – the letters of the alphabet. Different patterns of only 26 different letters give rise to a vast array of words, which in turn can be rearranged to give an even vaster array of thoughts, concepts and ideas, many of which are captured in literature.

Once again, we see that innovation does not require the 'invention' of new letters or new words: what it does require is the imagination to envisage new patterns – new arrangements of existing elements.

PAUSE FOR THOUGHT

One of the richest ways in which we create new patterns with language is through the use of 'figures of speech' such as simile and metaphor. Whenever we say 'he ran as fast as lightning' or 'he acted like a bull in a china shop' or when Dylan Thomas writes 'sloeblack, slow, black, crowblack, fishing-boat bobbing sea', we are using patterns at two levels.

The first level is that of the word, where the pattern of the words themselves has meaning; the second level is that of the mental picture – created by the juxtaposition of often surprising images.

Life

Look out of a window. What do you see?

If you are in a city you will see the urban environment, but you will also see some people. Each one of us is a distinct, different individual. Each one of us is a unique creation. Each one of us is a living instance of innovation.

If you are in the country, you can probably see plants, and perhaps some animals too – a huge variety of different individuals and different species.

Surely life itself is the most stunning instance of innovation on earth.

But if we look deeper, what is it that distinguishes you from me? A human being from a monkey? And from an ear of wheat?

Well, the difference between me and an ear of wheat is attributable to the difference in our respective genetic make-ups, as expressed by the chemical structures of the DNA contained within our respective genes. Each individual molecule of DNA is an extremely long chain of many millions, or even billions, of 'links', which, amazingly (with a very small number of exceptions), are of *only four types* – quite simple chemicals known as adenine, cytosine, guanine and thymine, as represented in Figure 2.3.

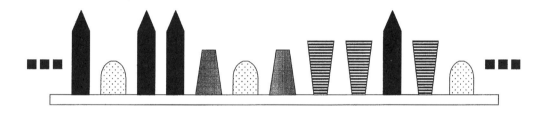

Figure 2.3   A representation of the structure of DNA

How many different sequences, or 'linear patterns', of these four links are possible?

Since each link can be chosen in any one of four ways, the number of different possible patterns for a chain of, say, 20 links is four multiplied by itself 20 times. This gives a total of 1 099 511 627 776 different patterns! And since human DNA consists of chains of literally billions of links, the number of different patterns is stupendously large – imagine (if you can) what four multiplied by itself a billion times represents. In practice, very many of these are biologically meaningless (just as many arbitrary combinations of letters fail to represent any meaningful words), but a sufficiently large number of meaningful patterns exist to explain why you, I and an ear of wheat are different.

So, just as innovation in music is attributable to different patterns of the same basic notes, and just as innovation in literature is attributable to different patterns of words, so innovation in life is attributable to different patterns of adenine, cytosine, guanine and thymine along our DNA molecules. It's all to do with patterns.

Yes, it works for business too

OK, it's quite entertaining to digress into music, literature and life. But what has all this got to do with business?

A lot.

Our excursion into music, literature and life has established that the fundamental basis of innovation is not the *de novo* creation of new building blocks; rather, it is the rearrangement of existing building blocks into ever richer patterns. If this is the case – as indeed it is for music, literature and life – then why shouldn't it hold true for business innovation too? In music the building blocks are notes, in literature they are words and letters, and in life they are chemical molecules and elements: for innovation in business, the key question must therefore be, 'In business, what are the basic building blocks that need to be rearranged in different patterns to promote innovation?'

What do you think?

The answer is closer to home than you might think.

For the answer is *you*.

The basic building block for business innovation is *you*, as expressed by your ideas and your experiences. And those of your colleagues too.

Business innovation springs from combining your ideas, intuitions and experiences with those of your colleagues.

Really. Think about it. And think about your experience of new ideas. Isn't that exactly how it works? Of course it is.

Up until now, though, your experience of this process of mixing ideas, intuitions and experiences is likely to have been accidental or haphazard. The trick is to make it deliberate, systematic and safe. To do this, we need to recognize that two very significant problems have to be overcome – one inside each of us, the other deeply seated in our mutual interactions . . .

The need for destruction

To recognize the first problem, which lies within each of us, we need to return to our examples of music, literature and life.

In music, we have seen that the difference between Beethoven's *Fifth Symphony* and *She Loves You* lies not in the invention of new notes, but in the creation of a new pattern of existing notes. Fine. But it is also true that you cannot create the new pattern of *She Loves You* by tacking a few extra notes on the back of Beethoven's *Fifth*. What you have to do is disaggregate Beethoven's *Fifth* back to its component parts – the notes – and then reassemble them in a new pattern.

The same applies to literature. You can't create *The Grapes of Wrath* by adding a few words on the back of *Hamlet*; what you have to do is disaggregate *Hamlet* back to its component parts – words – and then rearrange them into the new pattern.

And, naturally, the same applies to life too. You don't create a new organism by tacking some extra bits on to the end of some existing DNA: when an individual makes an egg or sperm cell, the two DNA strands inherited from each parent physically break and then recombine to form a new sequence of genes, ready to be passed on to the next generation.

So, the same must apply to business innovation too. If the basic building blocks for business innovation are expressed in terms of the experiences and ideas of you and your colleagues, these ideas and experiences come, not in their basic elemental form analogous to notes or words, but packaged together in more complex structures analogous to symphonies and novels. But if we are to innovate in business, we must firstly disaggregate our experiential 'symphonies' and 'novels' back to their component parts. We must destroy before we can rebuild.

PAUSE FOR THOUGHT

Most people find it very startling that innovation is a process in which our ideas are first disaggregated and then rearranged into new patterns. There are, however, two very familiar contexts in which we all have direct experience of exactly this.

The first is dreaming. All our dreams are composed of individual components which are immediately recognizable, but which have come together in often bizarre, even frightening, new patterns. This happens because, when dreaming, the activity of our censor of consciousness is suspended, allowing our

brains to roam freely, without the normal conscious constraints of 'sense' and 'logic'.

The second context is much more familiar, and very much less frightening – humour. Many jokes rely on an unfamiliar juxtaposition of two contrasting ideas, with the clash between them being relieved by laughter.

A man found a group of penguins roaming around a city street, and asked a policeman for advice. 'Take them to the zoo,' suggested the policeman. A few days later, the policeman saw the man once more, and the group of penguins was still with him. 'I thought I told you to take those penguins to the zoo,' said the policeman. 'I did,' replied the man. 'They loved it. And today I'm taking them to the cinema.'

I'm sure your jokes – and those of your children – are funnier than mine. But if you analyse how jokes work, you will find that almost all rely on the creation of an unexpected new pattern of familiar ideas.

From a business standpoint, of course, we cannot rely on the haphazard nature of dreams or the irreverence of humour. But we can exploit the fundamental process of searching for new patterns from existing concepts, experience and ideas. And we certainly can make this process deliberate, systematic, commercially sensible and organizationally safe.

Making innovation safe

To most people, the realization that innovation demands the disaggregation of our ideas and experiences is very surprising, even disturbing. And, even once that penny has dropped, most of us find the actual process extremely difficult – if not desperately so. Not only do we dislike having our basic experiences untangled (how dare you challenge my ideas?), but we have spent a lifetime developing strategies to avoid it, as we will discover in the next chapter. But before we do that, there is another problem we need to recognize . . .

Inevitably, the process associated with the disaggregation and destruction of our own ideas is intensely personal: not only is it strange, it can sometimes hurt. Consequently, we often seek to avoid it and are usually resentful when others try to 'help'. But if we sincerely wish to innovate and be party to innovation, we must be willing to disaggregate our own ideas and allow others to participate in the process. For, as the analogy with life might suggest, the process of combining ideas can be more fruitful – and fun – if other people participate. But, if done badly, the experience can be pretty awful.

So this second problem lies deep in ourselves, in our interpersonal behaviours, in the climate we create around the process of innovation, in the style we adopt, and in the way we interact with other people. And we come naturally back to many of the issues we discussed in Chapter 1 when we considered what makes an innovative environment. Clearly, if we have no idea where innovation comes from, or how to make innovation work, we will naturally be very clumsy at the process. But if we do have an understanding – as we are now gaining – we are in a much better position to create the environment in which innovation is not only safe, but fun too.

So, where does innovation come from?

To summarize. Innovation is born out of the rearrangement of existing component parts into new patterns: as Arthur Koestler stated in the quotation given at the start of Part 1:

> The creative act is not an act of creation in
> the sense of the Old Testament. It does not
> create something out of nothing; it
> uncovers, selects, re-shuffles, combines,
> synthesises already existing facts, ideas,
> faculties, skills. The more familiar the parts,
> the more striking the new whole.

The basic components, however, are usually packaged together into more complex structures which must be disaggregated before the process of innovation can take place. In business these complex structures are represented by our experiences, our ideas, our knowledge and ourselves. It is therefore not surprising that the process of disaggregation – the necessary precursor of successful innovation – can be so uncomfortable and disturbing. After all, we have all spent our entire lifetimes acquiring those experiences, forming our ideas, and gaining all that knowledge . . .

3 THE LEARNING TRAP

Make like a raindrop

Take a look at the map shown in Figure 3.1.

The map comes from a book, published in 1555, entitled *A History of the Northern Peoples*, written by the Catholic Archbishop of Sweden, Olaus Magnus. It is one of the earliest maps of Scandinavia and I find it very elegant. It also serves to encapsulate the take-home message of this chapter – a take-home message you will never forget.

So, make like a raindrop, and take a look at the next 'Pause for thought'.

PAUSE FOR THOUGHT

Look at the map, and find the range of mountains that runs more or less north to south on the border between Norway and Sweden. Imagine you are a raindrop, and that you happen to fall on the Swedish side of the ridge that lies along the spine of the mountain range. Choose a spot on the map where you fall. From that point, you will flow into a stream, and then a river. Will you arrive, in the first instance, in the Atlantic Ocean, or the Baltic Sea?

And what if you fell on the Norwegian side of the range?

We'll come back to the map shortly; meanwhile, think about the next 'Pause for thought' on page 23.

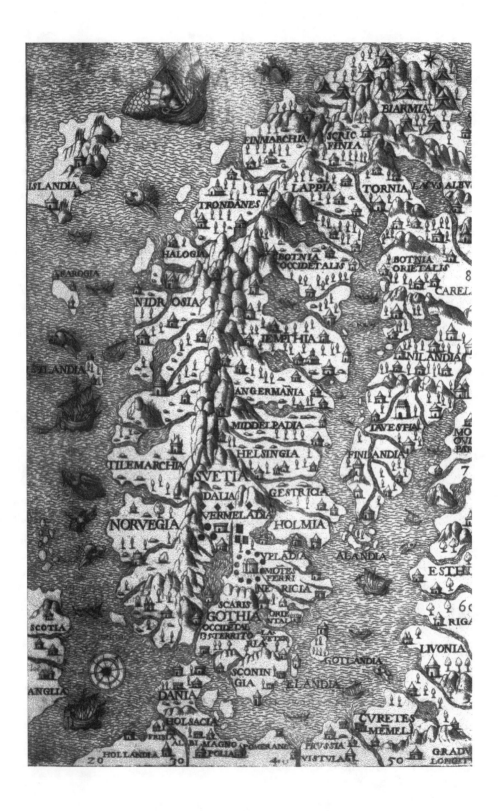

PAUSE FOR THOUGHT

How long, roughly, does it take you to get dressed in the morning?

(This refers to putting on your clothes only, not to other activities such as washing, waking up or deciding which clothes to wear!)

How many items of clothing do you usually wear on a normal business day?

(Count all items separately, so a pair of socks counts as two items rather than one; also, remember to include items such as a watch, spectacles and so on.)

And, in principle, how many different ways are there of putting on that number of clothes?

The dressing paradox

Most people get dressed in a few minutes – say, about five – and usually wear between eight and 14 different items, sometimes a few more or sometimes a few less, according to season. And the theoretical total number of different ways of putting on your clothes is shown in the following table.

Total number of items of clothing	Theoretical total number of different ways of putting on that number of clothes
7	5 040
8	40 320
9	362 880
10	3 628 800
11	39 916 800
12	479 001 600
13	6 227 020 800
14	87 178 291 200

Figure 3.1 A map of Scandinavia dated 1555 by Olaus Magnus
Source: *Danmark og det Øvrige Norden i Gamle Kort og Stik* by Eduard van Ermen and Erik van Mingroot, (1987), Borgen, Copenhagen.

Surprised?

Let me explain. Suppose you are wearing ten items. In principle, you have ten ways of choosing the first item, and so let's suppose you choose a sock which you put on your left foot. That leaves a pile of nine items from which you can choose the second item – say, a sock to put on your right foot. Given that you had ten ways of choosing the first item, and nine for the second, the total number (in principle) of different ways of putting on the first two items is therefore $10 \times 9 = 90$. This process continues for each of the remaining items, until you have only one left. So, the total number (once again in principle) of different ways of putting on ten items of clothing is given the multiplication $10 \times 9 \times 8 \times 7 \times 6 \times 5 \times 4 \times 3 \times 2 \times 1 = 3\ 628\ 800$. This number, by the way, assumes that all the items of clothing are the right way round and put on to the appropriate part of your body: if we allow for the possibility that a sock, for example, were inside-out or put over your hand rather than on your foot, the number becomes even more astronomical!

This number – in excess of three million – represents a theoretical maximum, for many of the combinations included within this total correspond to rather unconventional modes of dress – most of us, for example, have our shoes outside our socks. That's why the table refers to the '*theoretical* total number of different ways of putting on that number of items of clothing'. Nonetheless, if we confine ourselves only to realistic outcomes and socially acceptable dress options, the total number of different ways of putting on a normal number of clothes is still very large indeed, running into several thousands! Think about it: left sock before right sock, or the other way about; underpants before or after vest. You get the idea.

Out of the theoretically millions of different ways of getting dressed, only a few thousand correspond to a socially acceptable end-result. Getting dressed in the morning therefore resembles a puzzle which has several million possibilities of which only a few thousand give a 'correct' answer. The probability of finding a 'correct' way of getting dressed, simply by chance, is therefore approximately 1000 (a sensible estimate of the number of correct results) divided by approximately 4 000 000 (a sensible estimate of the total number of possibilities for ten items of clothing), or less than one in a thousand. These odds are considerably better than those of the National Lottery, but are still pretty small.

Given that getting dressed probably takes you only a few minutes each morning, how come you get dressed so fast?

This is the 'dressing paradox'. Every morning – just when we are at our most alert, of course – we have to solve the problem of how to get dressed. Assuming that our clothes have been laid out, and that we don't have to rummage through drawers to find them, we are faced with a jigsaw puzzle with millions of possible combinations, from which we have to choose one of a relatively small number of right 'solutions'. If we were to choose in which sequence to put on our clothes by trial and error, it would take us ages to hit on an outcome that worked – as, indeed, anyone who has helped a young child to get dressed knows all too well. How, then, do we get dressed so quickly?

The answer, of course, is that we do not solve the problem anew each morning. We have *learnt* the solution. So, each morning, we simply repeat our learnt, and probably identical, solution – I, for example, am a left sock before right sock man, every day.

Whack Pack!

Give yourself a whack on the side of the head

The more often you do something in the same way, the more difficult it is to think about doing it in any other way. Break out of this 'prison of familiarity' by disrupting your habitual thought patterns.

Write a love poem in the middle of the night.
Eat ice cream for breakfast.
Wear red socks.
Visit a junk yard.
Work the weekend.
Take the slow way home.
Sleep on the other side of the bed.

Such jolts to your routine will lead to new ideas.

How can you whack your thinking?

The power of learning

Learning is an immensely valuable experience. After all, why solve the same problem from scratch every time it is encountered? If – as the 'dressing paradox' illustrates – we can learn a solution, the time invested in learning it can be recouped many times over in time saved later on.

And it's not just a question of saving time – very often, it's a question of survival.

Take, for example, the problem of crossing a road.

As we stand on the kerb wondering whether or not it is safe to cross a busy road, we have to solve a problem of enormous complexity. We have to assess the positions and speeds of many vehicles; we must estimate the distance from where we are standing to the other side of the road; we need to take account of weather conditions; we do some very agile estimates of how long it will take us to cross in comparison with how much time it will take for that big bus to bear down on us; we also use our ears to detect sounds made by vehicles that might be coming, as yet unseen, around corners. The amount of information we need to process to solve the problem of crossing the road far exceeds the current abilities of computers and robots, yet it is a problem that we routinely solve day after day, almost unconsciously. But we do not solve this immensely complex cognitive problem each time we encounter it; rather, having learnt how to solve the problem during our childhood, we rely on this learning to keep us safe thereafter.

What is learning?

Let us now return to Olaus Magnus's map. As you will recall, the first 'Pause for thought' in this chapter asked you to 'make like a raindrop', and imagine what would happen if you fell somewhere on the Swedish side of the mountain ridge which forms the border between Norway and Sweden. Very probably the spot where you chose is unique – just as in a 'spot the ball' competition. But if, as requested, your spot is to the eastern side of the mountain ridge, you – and everyone else – will have given the same answer to the question 'Will you arrive, in the first instance, in the Atlantic Ocean, or the Baltic Sea?'. You all will have agreed that you would arrive in the Baltic.

By the same token, any raindrop falling on the western side of the mountain ridge would soon find itself in one of Norway's short, fast-flowing torrents, leading to one of the fjords and the Atlantic Ocean.

If we stand back from the specifics of a given raindrop, we can now appreciate that the physical geography of Norway and Sweden acts as a mechanism to transform multiple inputs (the positions of each of the falling raindrops) into just one of only two possible outputs (the Baltic or the Atlantic). While this is mildly interesting in its own right, it is far more interesting to surmise how, geologically, this might have been brought about.

The specifics of Scandinavia's geological history don't actually matter. What does matter is a 'thought experiment' that starts with Scandinavia as a flat, featureless plain in which a raindrop remains wherever it lands until it evaporates or is consumed by whatever life forms happen to be around at the time. At some time, a geological event occurs which raises the land somewhat along the line of what is now the north–south mountain range. Rain falling now will flow one way or the other depending on which side of the central ridge it lands. Initially, any raindrop will slide down one or other of the two smooth slopes but, as it does so, it starts to carve a valley. And as more rain falls, the existing valleys attract more drops, which in turn carve the valleys more steeply, which serves to attract more rain. Furthermore, as the land at the ridge rises, the valleys become increasingly well defined, until the landscape we see today is created.

The key point is that, as the valleys begin to form, the very existence of the initial, gently carved valleys attracts more and more rainwater to reinforce their shapes. The system becomes 'self-organizing' in that an initial, perhaps accidental, aspect of organization – the initial pattern of shallow valleys – progressively reinforces itself to become an increasingly strong feature.

Rain falling on a landscape, however, is not the only example of a self-organizing system: in 1949, the Canadian psychologist Donald Hebb published a book entitled *The Organisation of Behaviour* in which he hypothesized that learning – the imprinting of patterns of behaviour on the brain – is an analogous process.

Imagine the mind of the newborn infant as a plain, just like the imaginary plain of proto-Scandinavia all those millions of years ago. As the infant perceives the world, she receives inputs from her eyes, her ears and her senses of touch, taste and smell. Each of these perceptions causes some of the neurons in her young brain to send signals to one another. Initially, her actions, and the corresponding signals in her brain, are random. Suddenly, she discovers a particular sensation which she enjoys – perhaps the taste of her mother's milk – and instantly there is a spontaneous coordination across her senses of sight, taste, smell and touch, as well as with the sucking action of her mouth, all of which are associated with the actions of the corresponding sets of neurons. Some time later, at her next feed, she enjoys the same pleasurable sensations and the same sets of neurons are activated. Hebb postulated that the repeated activation of the same sets of neurons strengthens their mutual interconnections, thereby increasing their ability to act together again. This progressively reinforces these particular sets of neurons, and the associated behaviours so that, over time, the infant becomes increasingly more adept at coordinating her senses and her physical actions. The baby is learning.

Just as an increasing number of raindrops on early Scandinavia carved the valleys more deeply, an increasing number of reinforcing sensations builds stronger and stronger neural networks in the infant's brain. Hebb's great insight was to suggest that the brain, like the landscape, is a self-organizing system: as we learn, we reinforce particular networks of neurons, thereby correlating and coordinating sensory perceptions and physical behaviours with the activities of the appropriate sets of brain cells. As we learn, we carve increasingly deep 'valleys' in our minds, and so the 'plain' of the newborn infant becomes 'eroded' into the Alp-like landscape of the adult. This is the explanation for our expertise at getting dressed and crossing the road. We know how to navigate the 'getting dressed' valley each morning, and, as regards crossing the road, the complex sensory input experienced as we stand on the kerb may be likened to the pattern of raindrops on Scandinavia – the patterns are all different, but that is not the point: the point is how all those different input patterns can be transformed into just one of two output responses – 'safe' or 'unsafe'.

The hypothesis also offers an explanation for the effect of some drugs. Drugs act by chemical action, and it might be that certain drugs can influence large tracts of our mental 'landscape': just as an earthquake can disrupt the positions of geological mountains and valleys, so certain drugs might distort our mental 'mountains and valleys' giving rise to new mental pathways that manifest themselves as hallucinations or other strange effects.

In fact, in 1949 when Hebb first published his idea that the mind is a self-organizing system which becomes reinforced by learning, the term 'self-organizing' had not yet been coined, and there was only limited knowledge on the detailed cell structure of the brain. But today, the situation is quite different. First, the concept of the self-organizing system is well established and is a major component of 'complexity theory', one of the new branches of science which deals specifically with large-scale complex systems such as living organisms and societies. Second, our knowledge of the brain and its workings is much richer. In particular, the Nobel prize-winning biologist, Gerald Edelman, has demonstrated how self-organization can arise in computer simulations, and similar concepts are invoked by some of today's leading researchers such as Francis Crick and Stephen Rose.

CASE FILE

Self-organizing systems

Imagine grains of sand falling one by one on to the floor. At first, they form a neat cone but, suddenly, there is an avalanche. When the grains have settled, the underlying shape of the cone remains. And, as more grains are poured on, the sequence of growing a cone, followed by avalanche, continues. What is surprising is that the shape of the cone after all the avalanches is the same. Despite the randomness of the movement of the individual grains, the overall shape of the base cone is maintained. The system is self-organizing.

On a vastly different scale is the planet Jupiter. In Jupiter's atmosphere, plainly visible from Earth, is the 'Great Red Spot': a region of immense underlying turbulence, but with an overall, stable pattern. Another self-organizing system.

And on a different scale again there are the self-organizing systems of the stripes on a zebra, and of the beating of our own hearts. These are two more examples where apparently random underlying microscopic molecular events spontaneously and naturally show macroscopic structure, order, regularity, rhythm, stability.

Could life itself be a self-organizing system? And what about the behaviour of groups, organizations, societies?

The learning trap

The analogy of Olaus Magnus's map beautifully captures the principal message of this chapter – that learning is a process of carving 'valleys' in our mental 'landscape'. But it also captures a second great insight. If learning is about the process of 'flowing down valleys' – and the more quickly we can do this, the more quickly we can respond to a given set of external stimuli – then what does this imply about innovation?

Innovation, by definition, is a process of *not* flowing down those valleys! If we want to do known things differently, or to do new things altogether, the last action we want to take is to zoom down one of the valleys we have already learnt. We want to explore new valleys, or to sit astride one of the ridges or mountain tops and look around before we decide which new valley to explore. Yet our whole upbringing, our whole educational process, our entire experience of what is 'right' and 'wrong', of what is 'safe' and 'dangerous', has been conditioned by the existing valleys, as the next 'Pause for thought' amply demonstrates.

PAUSE FOR THOUGHT

What are the two missing items in the following sequence?

w   x   y   ?   ?

Well, that was easy wasn't it? Obviously, the right answer is 'z' for the first item, and 'a' for the second – clearly the sequence is just cycling through the alphabet, and having reached 'z', we need to go back to 'a'. Of course.

But suppose we are regular users of spreadsheet software – computer programs that enable calculations to be carried out as if on tabular paper composed of a network of rows and columns. In a conventional spreadsheet, the rows are numbered serially 1, 2, 3 . . ., and the columns are labelled with letters A, B, C . . . But when a spreadsheet reaches column Z, it usually continues AA, AB . . . So might the 'right' answer be 'z' followed by 'aa'?

But what about a sequence 'w, x, y, f, n'?

'Crazy', I hear you say.

Really?

Suppose the 'w', 'x', and 'y' were generated randomly, but just happened to be in sequence. If the 'w', 'x' and 'y' are random, so are the 'f' and the 'n'.

I showed this puzzle to my wife, who is Danish.

'Silly man,' she said. 'The answer's obvious: "z", then "æ".'

'æ'?', I said.

'Yes,' she replied. ' "æ". Danish has three extra vowels – "æ", "ø" and "å". In a Danish dictionary, "æ" follows "z". '

'Ah.'

How many other sequences can you think of?

So, next time you do an IQ test to fill in the gaps in a sequence, or find the odd man out or whatever, remember the learning trap. Maybe the identification of the 'right' answer is more a reflection of the question setter's limited imagination, experience, cultural background or capacity (or rather incapacity!) for innovation than your level of 'intelligence'!

Given the enormous influence of our whole educational system in bludgeoning us into the mind-set that there is only one 'right' answer, how on earth can we 'unlearn'? How can we bring ourselves into a condition for which we can innovate? How can we drag our 'raindrop' out of a valley and back to the top of the ridge?

This, of course, is why many of us find innovation so uncomfortable and so strange.

Innovation goes against all our learning. As it must. And many of us find this desperately, desperately difficult. We are so used to flowing down the valleys, to letting the raindrops go with the flow, that we have forgotten how to drag those raindrops back uphill, and we feel deeply uncomfortable as those raindrops teeter on the edge of a precipice, not knowing which way to fall down. But only by falling down a new valley will we come up with a new idea; only by making this happen can we deliberately, and systematically, innovate.

But now we know the secret. The details of neurophysiology need not concern us, for it is the analogy with the raindrop in the valley which opens our eyes to the need to think in a different way if we are to innovate. If 'traditional thinking' is the conventional method of allowing us to navigate the valleys, then a new way of thinking must be required to facilitate innovation. This is what Arthur Koestler, in his wonderful book *The Act of Creation*, called 'thinking aside' and what, a few years later, Edward de Bono termed 'lateral thinking' – a phrase that has now entered mainstream language. Both refer to the same need – a method of thinking to help your mind drag those raindrops to the tops of the ridges, so that they will fall down different valleys, thereby generating new ideas. We will discover some tools and techniques to help us do just this in later chapters but, for the moment, let us enrich our understanding of the great difficulty most of us have in 'unlearning'.

The simplest possible shape

Sam opened the envelope. Inside was a second envelope, and a sheet of paper. On the paper was written:

- Do not open the inner envelope.
- Give it to Chris.
- Await further instructions!

Sam handed the inner envelope to Chris, and duly awaited further instructions. Chris opened the envelope and beckoned Sam forward.

'What I'd like you to do, Sam', said Chris gently, 'is this. Just come to the front of the group, and stand by the overhead projector. In this envelope, I have several simple shapes. All you have to do is to put the individual shapes together to form the simplest overall shape. And so that everyone can see, I suggest you place them on the overhead projector. Is that OK?'

Sam nodded, but couldn't help feeling nervous. He hated standing in front of the group, and hoped he wouldn't make a fool of himself. Still, Chris was being reassuring, and all the exercises they had done so far had been quite safe.

'This is the first shape,' said Chris, handing Sam a rectangle some three inches long and one inch wide. 'Just put it down on the projector . . . Yes, that's fine.'

'And this is the second,' continued Chris. 'Where would you like to put it to form the simplest overall shape?'

Chris handed Sam a square, about one inch by one inch. Sam looked at it for a moment, and then placed it at the end of the rectangle, elongating the original rectangle by a further inch.

'That's fine,' said Chris reassuringly. 'You've made the simple shape of a long rectangle.' Turning towards the group, he then asked, 'What do you think? Is that a simple shape?'. The group nodded accordingly.

'Here, then, is your next shape,' said Chris giving Sam another rectangle, two inches long by one inch wide. Getting the hang of what was going on, Sam quickly put this third piece on the end, elongating the rectangle even further.

'That's fine,' continued Chris. 'And here is your last piece.'

This time, Sam looked a bit puzzled, for the last piece was L-shaped, with the cut-out being about an inch square. It didn't seem to fit very easily, but after a few exploratory trials, Sam placed the L-shape at one end, to give the result shown in Figure 3.2.

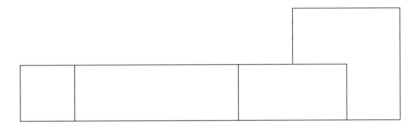

Figure 3.2 Sam's final shape

'Thank you, Sam,' said Chris. 'Please return to your seat. Thank you.'

As Sam poured himself a glass of water, he felt relieved that the ordeal had not been too painful. That last bit, though, was a bit of a problem. Never mind. Where else could it fit?

'Who has envelope B?' asked Chris, looking around the room.

'Me!' said Alex, as she opened the envelope, and found within it a second envelope which she then gave to Chris.

'This is very similar to the last exercise, Alex,' explained Chris. 'As before, I will give you a sequence of shapes, and all you have to do is put them together to form the simplest overall shape. Just as Sam did.'

Chris gave Alex the first shape – an L – which Alex placed in the middle of the overhead projector.

'Fine. Here's the second shape,' said Chris.

This second shape was a one inch square: a square that fitted neatly into the cut-out of the L, so forming a square about two inches by two.

'And here's the third piece,' continued Chris, giving Alex a rectangle, two inches long and one-inch wide.

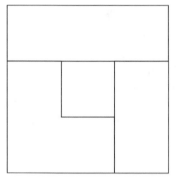

Alex immediately placed the rectangle along one side of the square, making a new rectangle, three inches long by two inches wide.

'And here's the last piece.'

This was a rectangle three inches long and one inch wide, which Alex placed along the longer edge, to form a three-inch square as shown in Figure 3.3.

Figure 3.3 Alex's final shape

'Thank you, Alex,' said Chris, and, turning to the group, continued, 'Let's talk about what has just happened.'

Unlearning is very difficult

I run this exercise – which, by the way, is based on one presented by Edward de Bono in his book *The Mechanism of Mind* – in all my training courses, and what I have described is a very common result. For, as you will by now have appreciated, the four shapes used by Sam and Alex were the same: the only difference was that they were presented in a different sequence. What happened?

In the first instance, Sam was presented with the shapes in a sequence such that the result, after the third piece, was a long rectangle of width one inch and length six inches. This was the 'right' answer at that stage (although other 'answers' are possible), for this is indeed the simplest possible overall shape formed from its three component parts. And when the last piece appeared, the L-shape, the most natural step was to put it on the end, as in Figure 3.2.

However, as was shown by Alex, the 'simplest possible shape' formed by all four shapes together is the three-inch square shown in Figure 3.3. Very few people form a 3×3 square as a result of the sequence experienced by Sam: indeed, most people end up with a shape like the one shown in Figure 3.2, or something similar. Why is this?

Well, the answer is threefold, and all three insights are fundamental as regards our ability to solve problems and to innovate.

First, the sequence in which information is presented conditions our answers.

In the first case, the sequence in which the pieces were presented conditioned Sam to think in terms of long, thin rectangles. When the last L-shaped piece emerged, this did not fit Sam's preconception of the pattern, so he did the best he could.

Yes, I agree that this is a trivial example, but how many times have you tried to solve a problem and been totally conditioned by the sequence with which you gathered information?

Second, to obtain the best possible answer to a problem, you must always, consciously, unravel, disaggregate and take apart your existing solution.

In Alex's case, the pieces were presented in a sequence which naturally led to the 'best' answer – the 3×3 square. This was not so for Sam. The pieces were deliberately sequenced to lead him down a blind alley, from which the only escape, when presented by the L-shaped final piece, was to take apart the long 1×6 rectangle, and reassemble the four pieces from scratch. A very few people do this spontaneously, but the vast majority of us do not. Some people explain this by saying that 'the rules did not permit it'. Really? What rules? The only 'rule' was the objective of forming the 'simplest possible overall shape' at each stage. There was certainly no rule saying that you could, or could not, take the pieces apart and rearrange them. Some notice the possibility of rearrangement, but choose not to do so, because this destroys the 'right' answer so far, and none of us like having our pet ideas challenged, do we? But by far the majority of us do not rearrange the pieces for the simple reason that we just don't think of doing it.

And, third, we must recognize that, while a problem is being solved, the current state of the solution is inevitably wrong.

Many detective novels are based on this principle – how often does Inspector Morse, with impeccable logic, suspect an innocent whose guilt is so consistent with the clues available at the time, but whose innocence is proven only when the last clue is found and a new pattern of evidence formed? And most Perry Mason stories hinge on the possibility of more than one explanation fitting any observed set of circumstances.

Yet how often do we recognize this principle ourselves? How often are we convinced we are right? How often do we ignore new information because it doesn't 'fit'? Or brutally force bits of information together even when we can see plainly that they don't? How often do we shout down a subordinate who has dared to challenge our ideas? And how often do we browbeat someone junior to ourselves for 'sloppy thinking' when they are quite clearly in the middle of solving a problem, and are still not only arranging and rearranging the jigsaw pieces, but also still searching for the pieces in the first place?

The 'simplest possible shape' exercise demonstrates a profound truth. Once we have learnt how to do something, it is very difficult to unlearn it. Yet unlearning must be a prerequisite for innovation. How else can we find a new shape if we are unwilling to disaggregate the existing shape? How can we find new ideas if we are unwilling to change our old ones?

CASE FILE

While a problem is being solved . . .

. . . the current state of the solution is inevitably wrong. Unfortunately, this uneasy state can last quite a long time, particularly if the innovation concerns the development of new products.

For example . . .

- In 1938, after several years of experimentation, Chester Carlson finally succeeded in making the process of dry photocopying – xerography – work. Over the following years, Carlson approached many blue chip companies with his idea, only to be turned down. Not until 1947 did he find support.
- The development of the float process for manufacturing glass took Sir Alistair Pilkington about seven years and nearly bankrupted his company.
- Around seven years was also the time needed by Howard Head to develop the use of metal for skis.

One of the most difficult commercial decisions is whether to prolong the agonies – and costs – of continued development, or to cut the firm's losses. No-one will ever know how many great innovations haven't happened because the development programme was terminated. To keep the development process going, you need a champion in the organization, and great personal tenacity.

Back to innovation

Well, what has all this to do with deliberate, systematic innovation? Let me draw the threads together.

One thread concerns the insight, explored in the previous chapter, that innovation involves finding new patterns of existing elements. But, as we saw when considering the examples of music, literature and life, before new patterns can be created, existing patterns must be disaggregated or torn apart.

The second thread, as explored in this chapter, concerns learning, or rather the state of having learnt. We have spent our entire lives learning, and many of us, particularly those of us who have been successful in the educational system and in our careers, have been very good at it. So, returning to the analogy of Olaus Magnus's map, we have a richly carved 'mental landscape', with well-trodden valleys through which we can travel really fast. This has equipped us extremely well to pass exams, to follow procedures and to do – quickly and efficiently – what we have done before. But these valleys constitute the precise antithesis of what we need to solve new problems, tackle new situations and do what has not been done before – to innovate.

So, to innovate, we must unlearn; we must get the raindrops out of those valleys back onto the ridges; we must unlock our minds. For, to form new patterns, to create the conditions which are logically necessary for innovation, not only must we understand the deadly nature of the learning trap, we must also be willing to see our ideas challenged, disaggregated, torn to shreds and ripped apart. If this process does not take place, we will be unable to rediscover the analogues of the elemental notes, words and chemical molecules so essential to innovation in music, literature and life. And if we don't break back to the component parts, we will never be able to reassemble and rearrange to solve problems creatively – we cannot innovate.

Because of the power of learning, and the deep love we have for our own ideas, most of us find the process of challenge, disaggregation and unlocking deeply uncomfortable. We are often unwilling to do it ourselves, and we can be bitterly resentful of others who attempt to do it for us.

Nevertheless, we must, and can, overcome these natural human inhibitions. The rest of this book will help, for not only will it introduce a range of tools and techniques specifically designed to unlock our minds and 'get those raindrops back on the ridges', it will also explore the issues of personal and interpersonal behaviour which can make the process fun (remember the example of life!).

But before we go further, let's 'Pause for thought' once more to round things off.

PAUSE FOR THOUGHT

Find a banana.
Eat it.
Enjoy!
(Or, if you don't happen to have a banana
to hand, think about what you would do if you were
to eat one.)

Well, I trust that was a good banana.

Before you eat a banana, you peel it, probably by holding the 'pointy' end, and breaking the peel back from the short stalk. Monkeys eat bananas too and, like their human relatives, they peel them first. But when a monkey peels a banana, she will most probably do it differently: she might well hold the banana by the *stalk* end, and break the peel back from the 'pointy' end.

This method has four specific advantages. First, it easier to hold a banana by the stalk, and when you peel it downwards, it comes out more cleanly. Second, inside the peel at the 'pointy' end is the banana seed. We humans usually treat this in a rather undignified manner (what do you do with it?); a monkey, however, genteelly nips it off as the peel is split. Third, the peel often splits more easily from the 'pointy' end – how many times have you wrestled with the peel of an unripe banana that stubbornly refuses to split at the stalk? And, fourth, by holding the banana by the stalk, you can eat the very last piece with dignity.

So, peeling a banana from the 'pointy' end while holding the stalk is manifestly better than the way we normally do it. Try it if you don't believe me.

Why, then, do we peel bananas from the stalk? Presumably, because we have always done so; because that's how our mothers and fathers always

Figure 3.4   Benchmarking banana-opening
Drawing by Barbara Shore

did so; because that's what we have been taught; because that's what we have learnt.

The moral of the banana story is therefore:

> **There is always another way of doing
> things, if only we can unlock our
> minds.**

Well, we've heard quite a lot about bananas, and we now know that innovation is all about patterns. Wendy Cope, in her poem *The Uncertainty of the Poet*, clearly empathizes . . .

PAUSE FOR THOUGHT

THE UNCERTAINTY OF THE POET

I am a poet.
I am very fond of bananas.

I am bananas.
I am very fond of a poet.

I am a poet of bananas.
I am very fond,

A fond poet of 'I am, I am' –
Very bananas,

Fond of 'Am I bananas,
Am I?' – a very poet.

Bananas of a poet!
Am I fond? Am I very?

Poet bananas! I am.
I am fond of a 'very'.

I am very fond of bananas.
Am I a poet?

Wendy Cope
Source: *Serious Concerns*,
Faber and Faber Limited, London, 1992.

PART 2

IDEAS

This is the great challenge for every organization: How do we come to know what we don't know? How can we identify, and then transcend, the boundaries of our knowledge?

(Gary Hamel and C.K. Prahalad, *Competing for the Future*)

4 GENERATING IDEAS

Mike's first brainstorming session

Mike was really pleased to have received the memo. He'd only been with the company five weeks and he didn't know many people yet, but there, on his desk, was the invitation to participate in a 'brainstorming session to generate new ideas for the sales ordering process'. Great. Just the sort of opportunity he'd been hoping for. And he was particularly excited to see who else had been sent a copy of the memo, and had been invited along too: not only the IT Director, his ultimate boss, way, way up the tree, but also the Sales Director, and the senior logistics manager. He'd not met these big-wigs yet, so he relished the thought of his first opportunity to shine. Not that he wanted to be pushy or aggressive – he recognized that, as a new employee (and a rather junior one too), he would be a very small fish in a rather big pond. But at least the pond would not have any sharks in it: during his interviews, everyone had been very relaxed and informal; first names were used quite unselfconsciously; and everyone, but everyone, had gone on about the importance of teamwork and of being flat-structured. Of course, Mike also appreciated the need to engage his brain before opening his mouth at sessions like this but, on this score, he felt pretty comfortable. In his previous job, he had been the team leader on a very successful sales order processing project, one that had been regarded throughout the industry as a benchmark – indeed, it was this very experience that was the major factor in his being offered the new job, and the promotion that went with it, here.

Mike gathered his papers, and went to the lobby to wait for the lift to the eleventh floor conference room. As he waited, he saw Chris, one of the senior sales department managers, coming towards him. Mike had spent some time with Chris getting an understanding of the user requirements for the new sales order processing system, and he'd seen Chris's name on the invitation list: Chris was probably on her way to the brainstorming session too. As Chris approached the lift, Mike looked towards her intending to say 'hello', and was about to do so, when he sensed that Chris just wasn't making eye contact. Feeling uncomfortable, Mike turned away and rummaged through his papers. And he felt even more uncomfortable when the lift duly arrived, the doors opened, and they both entered: it felt strange to be so close to someone he knew, in the claustrophobic confines of a lift, and yet not acknowledge the other's existence. As the junior, Mike felt he couldn't initiate the mutual 'good morning', which is why he had tried to make eye contact in the first place. But Chris had continued to avoid it, even when Mike had stepped aside to allow Chris, as his superior, to enter the lift first. Fortunately, the lift was rather crowded, so Mike was able to stand with his back towards Chris and so avoid any further embarrassment. Oh well, some people are like that I suppose, he thought. No point in getting paranoid.

The lift stopped at the eleventh floor and, without turning towards Chris, Mike stepped out and went straight towards the conference room. The room was large, with a splendid view over the City from its panoramic windows. Usually used for entertaining clients and guests, the room was rarely available for internal meetings. The centre of the room was occupied by a carefully maintained rosewood table – no coffee rings in sight – surrounded by about 30 chairs. Mike was feeling a little nervous now, so he chose a chair quite close to the door, but away from the sideboard where the coffee jugs were standing – he didn't want to be pouring cups of coffee all morning.

As people arrived, clusters of conversations sprang up around the table, and Mike began to realize that there were very few people whom he recognized. No matter. A good opportunity to make new contacts. At 10.30 sharp Lisa, the IT Director, stood up.

'Thank you, everyone, for making time to attend this morning's session. As you all know, the objective of the session is to generate new ideas for the sales order processing system, so I've invited a range of people from different areas of the business with an interest in this problem. This is a brainstorming session, so there are no rules – just be as wacky as you want. I'll write all the ideas down on the flipchart. Who'd like to start?'

Lisa took the cap off a red felt-tipped pen, and stood to the right of the flipchart, looking at everyone expectantly.

Silence.

Or, rather, silence to a backdrop of some 30 people riffling through papers, clinking coffee cups, rocking in their seats.

'Come on, folks,' said Lisa gamely. 'I've never known a group of our managers to get together without making a lot of noise. Who'd like to start?'

More silence.

'Well, I don't want to hog the meeting', continued Lisa, 'so let me write a few thoughts down.'

She turned to the flipchart, and wrote:

More flexible
More user-friendly
Faster response times

People round the table nodded.

'Any more?' she asked.

Yet another silence.

Lisa looked around the table and tried to identify someone who was willing to talk.

'Simon. You're the main user of the current system, and I know when we've been talking you've been full of good ideas. What do you think?'

'Well,' began Simon, putting his coffee cup down clumsily. 'Yes. Well. What I don't like about the current system is the colour of the screens. I don't know who designed them, but he must be colour blind. I think we should change their colour.'

'Yes. Thank you, Simon,' responded Lisa, duly writing

Change screen colour

on the flipchart.

Mike looked around the room, noticing that people were becoming increasingly fidgety. In an attempt to catch Lisa's attention, he leaned forward and raised his right index finger.

'Yes – you over there!' called Lisa, clearly indicating that she did not know Mike's name.

'I was wondering,' said Mike hesitantly, 'I was wondering if the redesign of our sales order processing system gives us an opportunity to think about doing something quite different. For example, instead of having our sales clerks typing in orders at their screens in our offices, is it possible to have our screens in our customers' offices so that they enter orders directly? That might save us money, as well as making the process more efficient. It might even give our customers better service.'

'That's pretty crazy,' replied someone that Mike didn't know. 'What if they keep making mistakes? That will spread all sorts of errors through our systems, and cause almighty trouble!'

'I agree wholeheartedly with Angus,' chipped in another unknown. 'Not only that, but think of the cost. Who's going to pay for all those terminals? And what happens if the equipment – equipment that we own and that we are responsible for – is damaged by some stupid customer? We take all the hassle, and the relationship with that customer is damaged beyond repair. The idea's barmy!'

Taking care not to write anything on the flipchart this time, Lisa asked for more ideas.

'I don't like the current coding structure,' stated the person to Mike's right. 'It seems to be all over the place, with numbers and letters everywhere. I can never seem to remember which codes go with which products.'

Change coding structure

duly appeared on the flip-chart.

More silence.

Mike leaned forward again, and felt uncomfortable as Lisa's gaze scanned past him in her search for someone else. But no-one else responded, and Lisa was obliged to return to him. She raised an eyebrow quizzically.

'When I was with my previous company', said Mike, 'we redesigned our screens to help our sales order clerks provide a good service on the telephone. As well as providing space for order entry, the screen showed a sort of script – a series of prompts and questions to ensure the clerk captured all the right details, and to make the customer feel well looked after.'

'Our clerks are very well trained,' responded yet another nameless person. 'They don't need that kind of spoonfeeding.'

'Yes. We tried that sort of thing once before. Years ago. It failed disastrously. The screen was so clogged up with text, the response time of the system made the whole process impossibly slow.'

'Anyway, we all know that we're the best in the industry. We set the standards. The others all come to us!'

Mike moved his seat back from the table and, for the following hour, took great care not to catch Lisa's eye again.

Have you ever been in a meeting like that?

At some time or other you've probably done one of those puzzles in which you are shown a picture and you are asked to ring the ten items that are wrong or out of place. Well, the episode described above is a rather more

sophisticated example of the same thing. How many items can you spot
that are almost wilfully obstructive to the objective of the meeting – the
generation of new ideas? And although the story is, of course, exaggerated
– a caricature – how many of those items have you experienced in
meetings in your organization?

What can you do about it?

In this part of the book, we'll look at some of the ways in which ideas can
be generated and explored. This is indeed the heart of the book, for it is
here that we will examine the fundamental processes of creativity and
innovation. As we shall see, we will always be operating at two levels
simultaneously: at the level of the *technique*, by describing a number of
tools to help make the process of innovation more systematic and
deliberate, and also at the level of *interpersonal behaviour* since innovation,
in its early stages, is delicate, fragile and so very easily crushed.

Where do new ideas come from?

From you. From your experiences, your frustrations and your knowledge.

But, as we saw in Chapter 3, your experiences are complex, packaged
mixtures: for the process of innovation to be successful, you must allow
your experiences to be disaggregated, pulled apart. Remember, you can't
create *She Loves You* by tacking a few more notes on to the end of
Beethoven's *Fifth*.

And remember also that, however well educated and mature you are, your
experiences, your frustrations and your knowledge are finite, limited,
bounded. This means that, acting alone, your opportunity to innovate is
severely constrained. Step one in innovation is therefore the willingness to
accept that, yes, other people *do* – not might – have a useful contribution
to make. They can bring their ideas, their experiences, their frustrations
and their knowledge to the table and mingle it with yours. And out of that
interaction, something new may emerge. This can happen internally, by
discussion with colleagues; it can also happen by examining what is
happening outside your organization by means of your contact with
customers, suppliers, competitors, other businesses and the world at large.

However, it will only happen if you want it to – if you unlock your mind
to let it happen. And don't expect new ideas to blossom simply as a result
of putting one of your concepts alongside one of someone else's. The

process is far more subtle. What will happen is that an element, a small component, an underlying shadow, of one of your ideas will combine with a fragment of someone else's to create something which neither of you would have generated individually. Remember now the analogy with life: genetic information comes packaged as a sequence of genes strung along chromosomes – individual genes do not have a separate existence. But the key feature of the reproductive process is the breaking of the chromosomes so that genes that were originally packaged on either the mother's or the father's chromosomes mingle to create a new, mixed chromosome – the innovative chromosome of the child.

And just as most people find the mingling of genes to be a pleasurable human interaction, so the mingling of ideas and experiences can also be fun, if you let it. The analogy can (just about!) be pushed further: both interactions are deeply personal; require some exploration; can lead to mistakes; can be clumsy; can take time; might not always work satisfactorily; involve a mixture of give and take; work better with experience; benefit from knowledge of appropriate tools and techniques; work better when the parties know and trust each other well; can be ecstatic; can have longlasting effects; can cause great damage.

Gathering ideas from within – brainstorming

So, let's return to the opening episode and draw some lessons. First, let's consider brainstorming as a process. The objective of brainstorming is to allow a group of people to declare and share ideas in an unstructured context. The absence of structure, of direction, of a specific objective is generally seen as liberating, but it can run the risk of the session degenerating into a random walk. Personally, I see brainstorming as playing a valuable role in putting ideas and experiences on the table as a precursor to innovation and creativity: the benefit of brainstorming is to allow ideas to be expressed in a reasonably safe and unconstrained context, but this is not necessarily the same as deliberate, systematic innovation. In my experience, some time needs to elapse between putting existing ideas on the table and formulating new ones. A brainstorming session is therefore the first step in a richer process.

Many people are reluctant to express ideas – they may fear losing respect, being laughed at or being put down. A brainstorming session with no structure at all therefore runs a significant risk of prolonged silences, embarrassment and arbitrary wandering. To avoid this, I prefer to introduce a degree of structure, particularly at the start to get things going, and also during the session when the energy level inevitably drops.

Some thoughts. Most of the following suggestions are written from the standpoint of the facilitator or chairperson, but they apply equally to participants.

CONTROL THE SIZE OF THE GROUP

Eight to ten is usually about right – small enough so that no-one feels excluded or lost, yet large enough so that no individual is pressurized to be sparking all the time.

INVITE DIVERSE PEOPLE

The purpose of brainstorming is to share ideas and experiences, so invite people from as diverse a range of backgrounds as possible – different departments, new recruits, old hands. In particular, try to include someone with experience of the outside world as they very often bring a wealth of different ideas and experiences. A brainstorming session attended by clones of 'yes' men rarely achieves anything more than the endorsement of the ego of the convenor.

BE COURTEOUS

If the group is indeed diverse, it is very likely that the participants might not know one another. If you are the chairperson or facilitator, introduce everyone or, better still, invite the participants to introduce themselves – not just by name and job title, but also by stating some item of relevance, such as an appropriate experience or an initial idea. For example, I often start such sessions by asking everyone, in turn:

- to state their name and role
- to describe an innovation, idea or concept, not drawn necessarily from their work experience, of which they are proud
- to identify one aspect of the current business situation in which innovation would be beneficial
- to state what kind of climate or atmosphere they wish to help create for the brainstorming session.

Such an 'opening circle' does wonders for the atmosphere: it puts everyone on an equal footing; because everyone is obliged to speak in turn, each individual can break the ice in a safe way; the request for an innovation, idea or concept of which they are proud reinforces the positive message that, yes, you can generate new ideas and frequently reveals quite surprising things; and by asking for one opportunity in which innovation would be beneficial, people are able to express their pet ideas, and often come up with some very interesting observations.

Furthermore, asking each participant individually to make an explicit, public statement about the climate or atmosphere he or she wishes to help create defines a 'social contract' for the session. Most people respond with words such as 'constructive', 'active', supportive', 'energetic', 'challenging', 'enjoyable', 'hardworking', 'fun' and so on – I have never had an occasion when someone elects for 'boring', 'destructive', 'hurtful', 'dull' or any of a dozen other negative adjectives which unfortunately describe some meetings you might recognize. By giving each individual the opportunity to declare his or her own personal desire, not only is it established that everyone wants the same, but it also legitimizes the facilitator to intervene to bring the session back on course should it veer towards the destructive or the negative.

Most importantly, the circle encourages everyone to do the single most important thing in brainstorming, or indeed in any other group interaction – to listen. To pay attention to what someone else is saying now, rather than to what I want to say if only he would shut up.

KEEP THE SESSION BRIEF

I have rarely experienced benefit from a session of longer than an hour – people just run out of steam.

START WITH A BANG

The opening line 'Welcome, folks. OK, what ideas have you got?' is a good way to generate silence. When facilitating, I prefer to move straight from the 'opening circle' into a brief personal exercise in which all the participants are asked to spend no more than two or three minutes considering such questions as:

- If you had to design the perfect sales order processing system (or whatever), what would it look like? Try, if you can, to use pictures, not words.

- If a Martian were to land here today to observe our sales order processing system, and then return in three years' time, what would he see that would be different?

After a few minutes, participants can be asked to share their ideas, and this usually gets the session off to a good start.

BE POSITIVE

Nothing kills a brainstorming session more quickly than the word 'no'. Probably the most important role of the chairperson–facilitator is to prevent the wet blanket of negativity from shrouding the entire proceedings in gloom, and this can be done in three principal ways.

First, make sure that people don't evaluate too soon. So, during the introduction, you should make it very clear that its purpose is to explore and share rather than to evaluate or judge. Consequently, it is important for the group to agree that certain behaviours – such as making negative remarks or personal put-downs – should be prohibited for the duration of the session. Most people will willingly agree, and anyone who has strong convictions to the contrary has the opportunity to be heard. Make sure that you seek each individual's agreement, even to the extent of requesting that someone particularly intransigent should leave the meeting and express his or her own views personally later. An explicit agreement to the 'rules', witnessed by one's colleagues, is a strong personal motivator to keep to the rules while the session is in progress, and also permits others to intervene if they feel that the agreement is being broken. In law, the maxim might be *qui tacet consentire* – he who is silent consents. In business, my experience is the opposite: those who remain silent whilst others assent are usually plotting rebellion.

Second, as soon as the dead hand of 'No' is detected, intervene. In the spirit of not being negative, it helps if the policing of the rule is not in itself negative – a put-down. So don't say, 'That was negative. We all agreed not to be negative. You got that wrong,' or whatever. The same thought can be put over more constructively: 'That didn't sound very positive to me – can you think of a way of expressing a similar thought from a more positive point of view?' Of course, 'no' can be expressed in many different and subtle ways, so be alert for variants of the following:

- 'That's a good idea, but when we tried it before, it didn't work' (this being a variant of the more general 'Yes, but . . .').
- 'That's a great idea, but of course it's far too impractical . . . (or you won't get support, or it will cost too much . . .)'.

- 'I'm sure that worked very well over there; over here, though . . .'

Also, beware of the trap illustrated below:

> 'What about improving our sales order processing by putting terminals in our customers' purchasing departments?' said Mike excitedly.
>
> 'That's a really good idea. How might it work?' responded Lisa.
>
> 'Well, er,' fumbled Mike, nervously picking at his cuticles, 'I don't know in detail. I haven't thought it through yet. It's only an idea.'
>
> 'Mmmm,' said Lisa, casting knowing looks at her senior colleagues, and quickly moving on.

Third, have confidence in the fact that it is usually very easy to guide a group into thinking positively, almost without their knowing it. It just takes a little thought and preparation. Take, for example, the two exercises suggested earlier about drawing a picture and about the Martian. Both are positive, forward-looking, and encourage people to look afresh, perhaps from a different viewpoint. This is far more effective than getting people to list, for example, the ten things they don't like about what happens now. The emphasis is not on what doesn't work now, but on what might be different in the future. The word 'different' is important, for it carries no baggage of goodness or badness and no implied criticism of the status quo. A diverse group usually finds it far easier to agree on a vision of something different in the future than to agree on the possible reasons for change. Remember that there are always some people who will wish to defend the status quo and who will resist direct criticism, often on perfectly valid grounds. To focus on what might be different in the future, because circumstances have changed, is therefore much more effective and unifying than throwing bricks at the past. And, as a counter to 'Yes, but . . .', which destroys, encourage people to acquire the habit of saying 'Yes, and . . .', which builds.

KEEP THE SESSION ACTIVE

To keep the energy level up, keep things moving at a rapid pace. All too often, the initial surge of ideas peters out and everyone becomes progressively more embarrassed. So, have a store of activities or exercises that you can invoke when the pace naturally slackens. A particularly valuable technique is to alternate between group activities and personal ones: breaking the rhythm of a group process by asking people to do something by themselves for just a few minutes encourages each individual to take some ownership and to become re-energized, and also provides a new stock of ideas for the next group session. For example, suppose that a brainstorming session has been convened to discuss the sales ordering process. If the pace slows down, you might ask the participants to spend two minutes considering any one of the following:

- five good things about the current process, and five things that might be done differently
- five aspects of sales order processing that you have observed elsewhere
- five fundamental themes that should be incorporated if the process were to be designed from scratch, without the burden of the legacy of the existing process
- five attributes of the process that are perceived by the internal users of the process (for example, the sales order clerks)
- five attributes of the process that are perceived by the external users of the process (for example, customers)
- five measures of the success of the sales ordering process.

My obsession with the number five is clearly arbitrary, as is the specific context. The general message is simple: these themes are positive rather than negative and also encourage each individual to think for themselves, and focus on particular areas – especially those in which participants are encouraged to look at the process (or whatever) through the eyes of others, such as customers. They also provide a fresh stock of material to share with the group.

WRITE ALL IDEAS DOWN

The purpose of brainstorming is to capture ideas. So, write them all down – even if you do not personally agree with them. It is often the case that 'she who holds the felt-tipped pen wields the power', but if you are holding the felt-tipped pen, your role is one of facilitator, not censor. There are three good reasons for this.

- First, it is a huge put-down for the participant to see the facilitator write down other people's ideas, but not their own. It fuels personal and organizational paranoia, and is a strong disincentive for that person to participate further. After all, why bother if no-one is listening?
- Second, it breaks the rule of not being negative. To consign an idea to the oblivion of non-existence is the ultimate negative act.
- Third, you might be losing the very best idea that came up during the session. As we shall see shortly, an idea that initially seems utterly crazy might be just the trigger to something that is not crazy at all.

Given that few people – especially when using a felt-tipped pen on a flipchart – can write as quickly as people can talk, the facilitator inevitably has to paraphrase and abbreviate. Sometimes it is very easy to be confident that you have captured someone else's ideas in a few words; sometimes it is less so. A good facilitator therefore often checks back with the speaker: 'Have I captured your idea appropriately?' This gives the speaker the opportunity to clarify if necessary; it makes the speaker feel that he or she has been listened to; it allows the idea to sink in; it gives the facilitator a brief break from writing; and it also gives the facilitator an opportunity to turn towards the participants, re-establish eye contact, and identify those who wish to be, or should be, drawn into the discussion.

Expect to cover a lot of flipchart pages, write boldly and (if you can!) legibly. Once a page is complete, hang it so that it stays in view – ideas suggested ten minutes ago often trigger new ones, and this opportunity is lost if the flipchart pages have been folded over the back of the stand. Ordinary flipchart paper is notoriously difficult to tear neatly, so there is much benefit to be gained from using paper with perforated, easy-to-tear sheets; even better are those special whiteboards which incorporate a photocopier enabling A4 sheets to be produced automatically.

FACILITATE ACTIVELY, BUT LIGHTLY

Facilitation means just that – helping the session move along. It is not a licence for control freaks to dominate, nor for the facilitator to have, at last, the opportunity to get all his or her ideas on paper. Each facilitator will, of course, have his or her own style, and we have all experienced how well sessions can go with a good facilitator, and how badly with a poor one. The facilitator must keep everyone involved and engaged, so, if he or she notices that a particular participant has not contributed for a while, that person should be asked a direct question along the lines of 'What do you think, Andrew?'. This rarely causes embarrassment, especially after an 'opening circle': it will, much more probably, enable someone who might be relatively shy to articulate their thoughts in safety. The facilitator also needs to prevent particularly noisy individuals from commandeering the session for their own personal benefit: this requires assertive, but nonetheless polite, intervention such as 'Thank you for that contribution, Tara. Let's see what someone else thinks.'

LISTEN

Unfortunately, I have met many people who go to all types of meetings solely to deliver their preprepared speeches. Rarely do they listen. Apart from being a basic human courtesy, listening – and indicating also that you have heard and understood – is an absolute prerequisite for innovation. How can you add to the inventory of your ideas if you refuse to listen to other people's? Unfortunately, not listening can become a cultural norm. It is a very weird experience to participate in a group of non-listeners, all of whom are actively seeking to take the limelight and none of whom are paying the slightest attention to anyone else. Hardly the climate for innovation!

Some organizations have a peculiar habit of not listening to more junior people. Often, more junior people are recruited after a few years' experience elsewhere. They join their new organization bringing not only the enthusiasm of youth, but also detailed knowledge of how their previous organization operated in the context of their specific role. Yet, frequently, any ideas that more junior people might propose are either actively ignored – or, more likely, not explicitly sought. This is, of course, usually in complete contrast to senior appointments from the outside: the expectation of a newly appointed managing director is that a new broom will sweep clean, the assumption being that you only have authority to introduce new ideas if you enter an organization in a sufficiently senior role to wield power. It is a pity that so many organizations lose the opportunity to innovate simply because they do not listen to their more junior recruits.

END PREMATURELY

Quit while you're winning, as they say. Brainstorming sessions can be fun, generating lots of energy and ideas. Sooner or later, though, even the best sessions will peter out, and this inevitably leaves people with a feeling of anticlimax, even disappointment. It is far better, if you can, to end the session buzzing so that the participants leave on a high of excitement. They will be very likely to continue thinking about the issues for a long time after. In this way the participants will continue to feel positive about the session, and the prolonged attention that they pay to the ideas, even if only 'in the back of the mind', provides just the right degree of incubation for really good ideas to hatch. I appreciate that it's difficult to 'end prematurely', in that the right moment to do this can arguably only be recognized with the hindsight of having failed to do so.

In practice, of course, it is simply a question of anticipating and engineering the ending. If the session is going well, but you are running out of the allotted time, it is better to cut the session off while people are still excited, rather than overrunning until everything grinds to a halt, or people start getting anxious about their next task. But if the session is within its prearranged schedule and you feel the energy level flagging to the extent that you sense that the session will naturally end in about ten minutes' time, intervene by asking everyone to do a two-minute personal exercise. This pumps the energy level up, and also gives a moment or two to plan the closing sequence. After some brief feedback from the exercise, which maintains the energy level, launch straight into the close.

CLOSE WITH ACTIONS

It is normal, conventional good practice to end meetings with a succinct summary of what has been decided, leading to action plans as to who is to do what next. My experience of brainstorming sessions is that this generality is only half-true: yes, you should end with actions; as regards the summary, however, I am rarely able to do this satisfactorily, so I often no longer attempt it. The reason for this lies in the purpose of brainstorming: these sessions are held to generate ideas and thoughts; they are not held as a forum for focused discussion, leading to a well-defined conclusion or decision.

At the end of a brainstorming session, I am usually surrounded by sheets of flipchart paper, containing ideas and thoughts in no particular order. Attempts to structure the order there and then inevitably fail, largely because there is in fact no structure, nor should there be. A succinct summary is therefore often impossible.

Brainstorming is to generate ideas, not to evaluate or decide.

So . . .

- Control the size of the group
- Ensure diversity
- Be courteous
- Keep it brief
- Keep it positive
- Keep it active
- Write down all ideas
- Facilitate actively but lightly
- Listen. Listen. Listen.
- End prematurely
- Close with actions

So, how can sessions be ended in a positive, forward-looking manner, and what sorts of action should be agreed? Different facilitators will, of course, adopt different styles, but one technique that I have found particularly effective is to close by asking everyone to scan the ideas on the flipchart pages, and select just one that they personally are especially interested in or attracted to. I then go round the group to ask each individual briefly to state their choice, and to make a commitment to think about that individual item more thoroughly after the session. This 'closing circle' gives everyone a chance to speak, encourages people to make a commitment, and constitutes an initial 'opinion poll' on the ideas generated. Quite frequently, two or more people independently choose the same idea, and so it is natural to suggest that those individuals form a 'task force' to develop that idea further, and to feed back their findings at the next meeting. Then, having thanked everyone for their contributions, the action points fall out naturally as:

- a commitment by the facilitator to produce neat copies of all the ideas, and circulate them to all participants
- a commitment by the participants to continue to reflect on the ideas generated
- a commitment by everyone to meet again to take matters further, with the objective of distilling and refining the ideas generated in the first session.

Gathering ideas from outside – benchmarking

At school we are taught not to copy. In business, things are different, and we call it benchmarking.

Yes, copying what someone else does or, more subtly, using other people's experience to enrich one's own, and to add to the stock of ideas on which we can draw, is a major source of the elements of innovation. I am not, of course, advocating unethical behaviour such as industrial espionage; rather, I am pointing out that the world is a rich repository of experience, and much of this experience is potentially available to you without transgressing the law or an ethical code of behaviour.

Benchmarking is a fashionable topic: many books have been written about it, and many consulting firms earn fat fees midwifing benchmarking deals across various businesses. I don't want to rewrite these books here, but I would like to make some observations about what I believe benchmarking does and does not have to offer, some of the things to look out for when participating in benchmarking, and how benchmarking can contribute to innovation.

First, just to ensure we are all talking the same language, let me offer my definition of benchmarking: *the process of comparing like, or analogous, business activities.* This is a broad definition, focusing on comparison, permitting the comparison to be within a single business or across business boundaries, and allowing for some imagination as regards what types of activities might be regarded as 'analogous'.

In my experience, the most common driver which stimulates benchmarking is to 'do better', as captured in a thought of the type:

> As a business imperative, we need to
> improve the cost-effectiveness of our

mortgage processing (or whatever). One way of doing this is to improve our productivity, which is currently running at a rate of 20 new mortgages a day (or whatever). If only we could establish what our competitors achieve, this will give us a goal to strive for.

The basic philosophy underlying this is that knowledge of what competitors can achieve is likely to motivate an organization more strongly than a simple 'try harder' message from the management. And there is a lot of truth in this. So, the organization embarks on a programme of identifying similar organizations with a view to finding out what levels of performance they achieve.

PAUSE FOR THOUGHT

Which five activities within your organization would benefit from benchmarking?

Against whom would you benchmark each of these?

What benefits would you offer to each of the other parties in return?

And what benefits would you gain?

Are there any other ways of achieving your benefits, without benchmarking?

The most obvious similar organizations are, of course, your direct competitors, and we immediately hit the problem of confidentiality. If I believe that my mortgage processing capability is key to my competitive advantage, I will be very wary of sharing any information about it with you. Enter the consultants. One way around the confidentiality problem is not to reveal information to a direct competitor, but to reveal certain types of information to a neutral, non-competitive third party, which can act as a gatherer of like information from others in the industry who collectively form a benchmarking 'club'. Firms such as management consultants are clearly in a good position to act as the 'honest broker' to the club members, and the service they provide is the gathering of the raw data, and the construction of comparative reports which preserve the anonymity of the sources: they might, for example, produce a 'league table' of numbers, with no attributions, which is circulated to all club members. Each member will recognize its own numbers, and so be able to assess the extent to which they have to 'try harder', but no individual member can explicitly identify who is at the top of the league, or indeed at the bottom.

An alternative approach is to contact one of the increasing number of firms which claim to gather performance data from different industries, against which you can compare your own performance.

When embarking on this kind of benchmarking, there are a number of points to bear in mind.

DEFINITIONS

Central to all comparisons is the issue of definition: you cannot compare apples with apples until you know they are not pears. In practice, the problem of consistent definitions bedevils comparisons. In the first instance, people are usually surprised when they suddenly discover that their use of a term such as 'mortgage' is different from someone else's, the surprise originating, of course, from the fact that they have been using the term 'mortgage' in a particular way for years. So how is it possible for someone else to use the same term to mean something different? Can you imagine the conversation?

> 'Yes, I think it would be great for our two organizations to benchmark our mortgage processing activities.'
>
> 'I agree. That would be helpful to us too.'
>
> 'Roughly, how many mortgages a day do you handle?'
>
> 'About 60, on average. Of course it fluctuates quite a bit.'
>
> '60? Really? That's quite a lot. Quite a few more than we do in fact. I think we are around the 30 to 40 mark.'
>
> 'Oh.'
>
> 'That means our processes could be quite different if you have to cater for greater volumes.'
>
> 'Quite possibly. But now you mention it, we have a few different processes running in parallel. Mortgages against boats, for example, are handled by an expert team.'
>
> 'Boats?'
>
> 'Yes, boats.'
>
> 'Do you call lending against items like boats "mortgages"?'
>
> 'Yes, of course.'

'Really?'

'Of course. All lending secured against property is a mortgage.'

'Not in our organization. We use the term "mortgage" only for lending against buildings. We call lending against other forms of property – which in our organization is extremely rare – "specials".'

'Oh.'

'So your figure of 60 "mortgages" a day includes lending against all types of property?'

'Of course.'

'And of those 60, how many are specifically loans against buildings?'

'Well, er. I don't know offhand. I'm not sure. I don't think our systems . . .'

And that was an easy one. Imagine the fun you can have comparing definitions of items such as 'cycle time', 'failure rate' or, horror of horrors, 'quality'. Fundamental to any comparison is a full mutual understanding of the definitions of the items being compared, and it can often take a long, long time for definitions to be specified, understood, compared and rationalized. Anyone who has tried to compare published accounts will know exactly the problem here, even with such well-charted territory as 'sales' and 'depreciation'.

While studying definitions, don't be surprised if you discover that the same term is used with different meanings *within* your own organization – in different subsidiaries, branches, divisions or locations. Tidying this up within your own organization is, in fact, one of the hidden benefits of external benchmarking – the desire to compare externally drives the process of cleaning up internally. The computer department can usually help here, for one of the important disciplines in computing is the creation of standards, so that consistency is achieved in different locations and at different times. One of the most important standards is known as a 'data dictionary', a master list of definitions, used by the computer team to ensure that when any item is captured by a system and stored on a file, any other system using that item can do so in full confidence of just what that item is. In essence, one of the primary objectives in external benchmarking is to compile an agreed 'data dictionary' of all the items of interest – and the compilation of the dictionary is one of the tasks where external consultants can add real value.

The result of this will be a shared set of definitions. You should, of course, expect the shared definitions to be different, to some degree, from those currently in use in your own organization. You may use this as an incentive to change your internal definitions, but this can be a very complex task; more likely, you will need to define some process whereby your day-to-day data is transformed into the agreed format by some special process, carried out either within your organization or by the 'honest broker' consultants if they are used.

Which leads to systems. Every organization uses increasingly complex, integrated and ageing computer systems to process their data, and benchmarking usually places yet more demands on systems to do things differently. Much benchmarking soon becomes constrained by 'I don't think we can do that. Our systems don't . . .'.

And finally, of course, the problem of definition can be used as an unshakeable witness for the defence. What better way is there of explaining to your boss why it is that, according to the whatever-it-is performance measure, your organization doesn't quite rank as high in the league table as your boss would like? 'Well, of course. That's because we define it to be . . . whereas the others . . .' You know what I mean.

NUMBERS

'Giles, I've been looking through these benchmarking numbers. They're rather interesting. They've taken a bit of time to come through, haven't they?'

'Yes, they have. But we spent ages – much longer than I'd expected, in fact – agreeing consistent definitions, and then we had to have a whole host of tweaks to our systems. And some of the other participants in the club took even longer to get their systems up to speed. But I think we're all right now. Those numbers are pretty meaningful.'

'I see. Well, according to this table, the best-in-class is achieving a performance level of 62 mortgages a day, on average, but we can only seem to achieve 45. What are you doing to increase our productivity, by – well, it's about 40%, isn't it? If whoever it is can achieve 62, why are we only achieving 45?'

'Well, er . . . I'm not sure. It's a systems problem. Well, you know how we've been waiting for the implementation of our new image processing system to capture and handle the source documentation and, at last month's steering committee, that software house said they'd been delayed again . . .'

Another familiar story.

The point here concerns the value – or indeed otherwise – of numbers. Yes, league tables can show your position in the context of a defined peer group, and very nice it is too if you are at the top. If you are not, you know what you have to strive for. But the problem is *how*. What do you actually have to *do* to claw your way up the league table? This, of course, is not a question of *numbers*, but a question of the underlying *processes*. Maybe the others process more mortgages because they sell more in the first place. Maybe they process more mortgages because they have smarter systems and procedures. But the numerical measure of what *they* do is not the issue: the issue is what *you* have to do to make your processes more productive. And numerical benchmarking has very little to offer here. Knowing that you are umpteen per cent less productive than one of your competitors may provide the political will for change but, of itself, it does not address the central problem of *how* to change.

This in turn leads to an important and fundamental issue. Did you really need to go through all the anguish of numerical benchmarking at all? You have probably known for a long time that you need to increase productivity, and the key to do this is from the inside – by changing your internal processes and procedures. And after all the agony of getting comparable numbers from the benchmarking club, you still have the same need. Yes, it has been quantified, and there is a benefit there, and maybe some of the work that was done on unifying definitions and tidying up systems has helped too. But the fundamental issue remains. How to innovate. How to get new ideas. How to do things differently.

So, don't wander into benchmarking as an excuse to avoid the real problem.

And don't forget that while you are struggling to play catch-up, the leader is forging ahead too. If you are fortunate enough to be the leader, it is nice to know that you are on the top of the pile, but your motivation for change must surely come from within. Which is probably why you are on the top of the pile in the first place.

PROCESSES

So we arrive at the point that the real purpose of external benchmarking is not the sharing of numerical performance measures, but the prospect of understanding better how someone else's processes work. In short, to copy what they do. But if I believe that the design and management of my internal processes gives me competitive advantage, the last thing I will do is share that with you, my competitor. I might be quite happy to give you some of my numerical performance measures, and bask in the glory of watching your face turn green with envy. But let you know how I actually achieve that? Never!

The take-home message from this is not to expect competitors to divulge what they believe to be the secrets of their competitive advantage – just as you would not. To share information – to benchmark – at the level of the process, rather than at the level of the numerical performance measure, requires a deep mutual trust and empathy between organizations, and this takes a long time to build. Certainly, it can be done; but don't expect it to happen overnight. Also, expect such a relationship to be reciprocal: why should he show you his if you won't show him yours? Reciprocity, of course, is a question of perceived value, rather than like-for-like sharing. If I have a wonderful mortgage processing system, but yours is crummy, you gain a lot from looking at mine but I gain nothing from looking at yours. So no deal. While touching on the reciprocity issue, let me just note that there are some organizations that have done themselves long-term reputational damage by being well known for asking others for benchmarking data, but never releasing their own data in return. Word of this selfish behaviour quickly gets round the marketplace, and such organizations soon find themselves ostracized and shunned from any cooperative industry ventures.

This naturally leads to the concept of benchmarking, not against competitors but against an organization in the same line of business, but geographically remote or in a different line of business altogether, so that commercial confidentiality is not an issue. This works. Sharing with a geographically remote, but otherwise similar, business can be a very good opportunity for comparison, but it can become expensive; as regards different lines of business, the trick is to be ingenious enough to spot an industry from which there is something to learn, and to identify one or more players in that industry who not only have examples of best practice but would be willing to share, and to whom you can offer something of value in return.

One way of doing this is to identify process analogies. For example, in mortgage processing, a number of steps are involved such as capturing data from a variety of source documents, including legal agreements; checking various items for their validity, such as credit referencing, evidence of title and so on; risk management of the lending decision; and looking after clients during what, to them, might be a stressful period. Yes, all other mortgage processors do that too, but what other organizations have to do credit referencing? Or risk management of lending decisions?

Or complex document processing? Or maintain high levels of customer care?

What about credit card companies? Personal loan providers? Many government departments process large volumes of paper which require good indexing for fast retrieval. Many retailers, or those in leisure industries, have high standards of customer care. You never know in advance from whom you can learn. But you will, if you keep your eyes, ears and – most importantly – mind open.

And while you are keeping your eyes, ears and mind open, look around: life has some truly startling processes, and we have much to learn from those many living creatures which, over millions of years, have evolved ingenious solutions to very difficult problems.

Whack Pack!

Look to nature

The sticky hooked spine of the common burr inspired the man who invented the Velcro fastener. The 'spinning wing' feature of the elm seed served as a model for more efficient windmills and helicopters. Bell invented the telephone by imitating the ear.

What patterns and cycles in nature can you use to develop your idea?

Reproduced, with permission, from *Creative Whack Pack*
©*Roger von Oech. Box 7354 Menlo Park, CA 94026 USA*

So, in summary, be realistic about benchmarking. If you want to improve performance, one of the most powerful motivators might not be to benchmark externally at all, but to benchmark internally – to compare like departments within your own organization against one another. Since the span of the benchmarking is within a single organization, in principle, issues about definitions, systems and the sharing of best practice should pose no problems. But not always. I remember well one particular organization with which I had done some work improving their production scheduling. The assignment had been very successful, and I asked the factory manager if he would make an introduction on my behalf to one of the other factories in the group. 'No chance,' came his reply. 'We're in competition against them. No way would I ever share anything.' Oh well . . .

CASE FILE

The origins of the First World War

The historian A.J.P. Taylor argues powerfully that one of the causes of the First World War was the railway timetable: once Germany had begun to mobilize, the relentless rhythm of the railways moved so fast and effectively that there was no turning back.

The speed of Germany's mobilization was partly attributable to the efficiency with which they loaded their trains with heavy equipment. Rather than loading the wagons through doors in the sides, they loaded from the rear of the train, right through a network of interconnecting wagons – just like cars are loaded on the cross-Channel train, *Le Shuttle*, today.

The Germans adopted this method after a visit to Germany by Barnum and Bailey's circus in 1901. Having heard how quickly the circus loaded its trains, Kaiser Wilhelm II sent some senior army officers to see how they did it. They saw that the circus loaded its trains through the back, not through the sides. As a result of this benchmarking, the German army was able to load three trains, each of 22 wagons, in a single hour.

5 WHERE TO LOOK FOR NEW IDEAS

Exploring boundaries

'No man is an island' as John Donne would say. Unfortunately, in business, you sometimes come across a manager who is unaware of this: he or she sits on a private island of tranquillity, expertise and efficiency, surrounded by a furious sea of chaos, incompetence and profligacy.

Almost every organization is structured in terms of managerial fiefdoms, in which any given manager has control over defined resources. Some organizations represent the span of managerial control in terms of a hierarchical organization chart, in which the big boss has a number of immediate subordinates and so on to the bottom of the tree; others have more complex reporting relationships in which, for example, any one middle manager may be accountable to two or more higher-level managers – one reporting line might be geographical (to the manager responsible for the South, say), and the other might be functional (to the national sales manager). Whatever the organizational structure, and whatever the theory, in practice there are boundaries – boundaries which delineate the territories of adjacent chieftains.

One of the important insights of the fashionable subject of 'business process re-engineering' is that many business processes cross, and indeed recross, organizational boundaries. An archetypal example is the process of new product development which is, of course, essential to all businesses. Typically, new product development involves skills and resources from almost every functional part of the organization: the marketing strategists monitor the competitors and might spot new market opportunities; the sales force are in constant contact with customers; designers ensure fitness-for-purpose; production engineers determine how the new product can be manufactured; the accountants estimate product costs and assist with pricing; computer specialists design and build new systems; the personnel department might recruit new staff or train existing staff in new skills; lawyers might draft new conditions of business or contracts; property managers have a role to play if new premises are to be built. The list goes on. One of the outcomes of good process re-engineering can be a realignment of managerial responsibilities with business processes, and this can be beneficial. However, no single organizational structure can be perfect for all situations, and organizational boundaries will always exist. And it is those boundaries that are usually fertile hunting grounds for new ideas and innovation – particularly innovations relating to the very processes that cross those boundaries.

Why?

For two reasons:

- First, boundary zones are often blurred, and under no-one's specific responsibility. This no-man's-land is therefore likely to be poorly designed and managed.
- Second, study of a boundary is usually politically safer, particularly if the study is carried out by someone other than the territory's natural owner. Many managers – probably rightly – feel protective of their own patches, implying that a search for new ideas might be resented if it focused on their heartlands.

CASE FILE

Crossing the boundaries

Many innovations in business have occurred when an organization has chosen to cross boundaries. For example:

- UK insurer Direct Line leapfrogged over the boundaries of the traditional selling network of salesmen and insurance agents by introducing a telephone-based service to enable the customer to have direct contact with the company. This simultaneously improved customer service, cut operating costs, lowered prices and improved profits. A true win–win game.
- Supermarkets and major retail chains are crossing the boundaries between the traditional segments of consumer businesses by progressively extending their range of products and services beyond food and clothing and into financial services such as banking.
- Benetton achieved great success by crossing the conventional boundaries between purchasing, manufacturing and retailing. Traditionally, manufacturers of coloured woollen sweaters anticipated which colours would be in fashion next season, purchased the corresponding coloured yarns, and manufactured their stocks. But if their guess of next season's fashions turned out to be wrong, they would be left with great deal of unsold stock. Benetton avoid the need to guess next season's fashionable colours: they manufacture their entire stock in a single colour, grey-white, and then dye the finished garments at the last possible moment when they know what colours are 'in'.

The discussion so far has concentrated on boundaries within organizations, but an organization as a whole may also be defined by the boundaries between itself and the outside world – boundaries across which the organization interacts with customers, suppliers, the workforce, the local community, the media, government. Goods, materials, people, energy, knowledge and information continually pass in both directions across each of these boundaries, for the organization as a whole is no less an island than the individual. So, as with the organization's internal boundaries, a study of what happens at, and over, the external boundaries can trigger much innovation.

What do you find when you look at boundaries?

DELAYS, PILES AND QUEUES

Boundaries often give rise to delays, piles and queues. At a macroscopic level, think of the queues, and consequent delays, you experience when you cross a national boundary at the customs desk of an airport or at the border check point on a motorway. Closer to home, your boundary is your in-tray. How often is that empty? Identifying, and then removing, the causes of delay is inevitably fertile ground for innovation, and boundaries are the right place to look.

This is the concept of 'just-in-time' management in manufacturing industry. Rather than hold expensive stocks of raw materials and partly finished components in a factory, is it not both cheaper and more effective to have raw materials delivered just when you need them? Yes, of course it is. But how do you do it? By managing the boundary between you and your suppliers, that's how. Rather than being in an adversarial relationship with your suppliers, it is far better to work in harmony so that your requirements can be dovetailed into your suppliers' capabilities. That way, your suppliers can deliver just what you need just when you need it. The invention of the 'just-in-time' concept was innovation on the grandest possible scale.

And there are more prizes to be won. Which will be the first supermarket to find a really innovative solution to the problem of check-out queues?

KNOWLEDGE GAPS

One way in which you can discover how a process operates is to talk to all the individuals involved in it and ask them 'What do you do?'. The more people you talk to, the more the components of the process are uncovered, until the full picture is revealed. After you have done that, revisit various

people and, instead of asking the question 'What do you do?', ask 'What do you know about what Angela does?' (Angela being a person upstream or downstream in the process). Very occasionally, I have met the response 'Who's Angela?' (or whatever); more likely I
get something like 'Well, I'm not quite sure. I think it's something to do with . . .'.

With increasing specialization, people become increasingly focused on their own activities and have less and less experience of how their work fits into the greater scheme of things. This, too, is innovation territory. By sharing knowledge of what is happening up and down the process, individuals who may interact only rarely may discover ideas for improving the process overall. The most common example of this concerns filling out information on forms or on computer screens. Early in the process, someone might capture some particular item of information – for example, a code number for, say, a salesperson. The individual capturing that information has no idea why that code is used, but continues to enter it as it has always been so. Further down the process, you may discover that someone else erases that code because the system for calculating salespeople's commissions has long since changed. So, for a long time, someone has been laboriously looking up the right code and entering it, and someone else has been erasing it. A trivial example, I know. But the world is full of such oddities, caused by the lack of knowledge of the individual's role within the whole.

The issue of useful cross-boundary knowledge is much magnified across external boundaries. Do you manufacture goods in a particular packaging format only to have your customers waste time, energy and materials unpacking them, whilst thinking 'If only they could have packed it that way rather than this!'? What further opportunities exist to integrate your

CASE FILE

Art

The history of art shows many examples of innovation at the boundaries. As Arthur Koestler points out in *The Act of Creation*, the burst of artistic innovation in Greece in the sixth century BC took place at the mutual boundaries of the Egyptian, Oriental, Cretan and Northern tribal cultures; Tuscany, the cradle of the renaissance, lies at the boundary between North-western Europe, with its Gothic heritage, and the Eastern Mediterranean, steeped in the Byzantine tradition.

company's sales order processing routines with your customers' purchasing systems?

All these are boundary issues where the theme is knowledge of what happens on the other side: once again, as a place to look for the seed of innovation, a good one.

COMMUNICATION PROBLEMS

A variant on the knowledge theme is the issue of communications. In many ways they are similar, but there is one key difference. Knowledge about a process is inherently passive and impersonal, and implies being able to write the process down and maybe explain it coherently to someone else. Communication, on the other hand, is active and personal, and influenced by personalities. Even if organizational boundaries are blurred or eradicated, there will always be boundaries between my space and his. These boundaries are more subtle and political, but nonetheless real. Furthermore, it is these boundaries that become increasingly more strongly defended as one goes higher in the hierarchy.

An example. Strategy. Many organizations seek to develop a medium- or long-term strategy, and this is rightly a major preoccupation of senior managers, if not the very top. Some people see a strategy study as the search for the 'right' answer, or as a means of refereeing the squabble over the allocation of resources. Others see strategy as a vehicle for ensuring that everyone in the organization has a shared vision of the future, and that managers in their various roles are well equipped to deal with different situations as an uncertain future evolves, so that the organization is consistently steered in an agreed direction even if the wind, so to speak, begins to blow from a different direction.

This view of strategy as learning demands a high degree of trust, mutual respect and shared understanding among large groups of people, all of which is underpinned by open communication.

What has this to do with innovation? A lot – particularly in the context of knowing where to look. Organizations are organizations by virtue of the requirement for cooperation across a greater or lesser number of people, and this cooperation is achieved through communication. Communication only works, however, if the person who communicates does so clearly and, if the person to whom the communication is directed wishes to listen and to understand. The need for innovation may therefore not be in the content of the communication, but in the process of communication – the clarity of the message delivered, and the willingness of the receiver to hear it. It's all a question of boundaries.

Which leads naturally to the most significant boundary of them all . . .

The ultimate boundary

Your mind.

Let's pause once more for thought.

PAUSE FOR THOUGHT

● ● ●

● ● ●

● ● ●

If you haven't seen this puzzle before, can you find a way to join all the nine dots, using only four straight lines, and without lifting your pencil from the paper?

If you have seen this puzzle before, you already know how to join all the nine dots with only four lines. So, can you find a way of doing it with only one straight line (really!)? Or, rather, how many different ways can you find of doing this?

If the puzzle is new to you, do try it – don't give up: I know it's infuriating, but there is an answer. And you'll kick yourself when you see it. So keep going!

There are a number of different answers, all variations on the theme illustrated in Figure 5.1 on page 74.

As you can see, there are only four straight lines: starting at the top left, you first go directly to the right to a point beyond the top right corner, then diagonally downwards to the left to a point beyond the bottom left corner, then up to where you started, and then diagonally down to the right. Just four lines.

Many people find this puzzle very difficult, and give up in despair. Why? Because they try to keep their lines within the square implied by the outer eight dots. Having started at the top left corner, they join the top three dots, and stop at the top right corner. They next go down the right-hand side, along the bottom, and then back up the left-hand side to where they started. The four lines have been used, but the middle dot remains stubbornly unconnected. No matter where you start, or how you try to do it, you just can't find a way to join all nine dots with just four lines. Not by keeping within the square. The only way to solve the puzzle is to extend your lines beyond the corners – to 'think outside the box', as the saying goes.

Some people are surprised that you are 'allowed' to draw lines 'outside' the box. But who said you couldn't? Where did the implied rule that you had to keep within the box come from? Where was this assumed boundary specified?

Well, the constraint was the ultimate boundary – the boundary of your mind. If you, like many others, tried to keep your lines within the box, the only explanation is that your mind told you so – no-one else did.

As you can now appreciate, this puzzle is about two types of boundary: the physical boundary, implied by the eight outer dots, and the mental boundary imposed by your mind. Innovation, the ability to discover new ideas, is all about looking at the boundaries. And the most interesting boundary is the ultimate one in your head.

But what about solving the puzzle with only one straight line? 'Impossible,' I hear you say. 'Just impossible. It was hard enough to do it with four. But one!'

Well, here are five ways of doing it with just one straight line:

- Use a paint roller to draw the line. As long as the 'pencil' has a 'lead' wider than the length of the side of the square, then any line across the square will join all nine dots in but a single (wide!) stroke.
- Cut out the nine dots, and put them in a straight line; then join them up.
- Fold the paper so that the upper row of dots touches the middle row from above, and fold again so that the lower row touches the middle

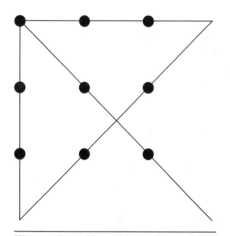

Figure 5.1 How to join all nine dots with four straight lines

row from below. This leaves a pattern of three 'fat' dots, which can easily be linked by a single, somewhat thick, straight line.

- Fold the paper so that the first column of dots lies directly over the second column, which in turn lies directly over the third. Then fold the paper down from the top so that the uppermost dots are in front of the middle ones, and fold the paper back from the bottom so the lowermost dots are now behind the middle ones. This organizes the dots into a single line, one behind the other. With a very sharp pencil, drill through the wodge of folded paper to join all the dots.

- Photocopy the puzzle using a reduction photocopier so that the nine-dot pattern is compressed to a small enough size to swipe once with a felt-tip pen. Then photocopy again, enlarging back to the original size.

I can hear the gasps of exasperation. 'That's not fair!' you cry. 'Who said you could use a paint roller? Who cuts up books? That wasn't within the rules!'

What rules?

I agree that cutting up books is not regarded as decorous behaviour in a public library, and relatively few of us carry a paint roller in our inside jacket pockets or handbags. But the question wasn't 'How can you join the nine dots with a single straight line in a manner that would not raise an eyebrow in a public library?', nor was it 'How can you join the nine dots using an implement commonly found in a lady's handbag?'. The question was simply 'How many ways can you discover of joining the nine dots with just a single straight line?'.

So, any constraints or rules were totally self-inflicted. They were all in your mind. So, once again, we are back to boundaries.

Challenging the rules

As these puzzles have demonstrated, the most difficult boundaries to surmount are those in our minds, particularly those that relate to 'rules'. Since our childhood, we have been taught to behave within the rules: that this is 'right' and 'good'; that behaviour outside the rules is 'wrong' and 'bad'. For sure, legally and ethically, this is correct. But we have become so used to operating within the rules that we impose all sorts of rules on ourselves that just aren't there. And if scanning the boundaries in general is the right place to train our binoculars when searching for opportunities for innovation, focusing on the 'rules', both the real ones and the imaginary ones, can yield very exciting results.

Where are these rules? Well, every organization is stuffed absolutely full of gently grazing sacred cows, of unwritten assumptions. Many of these are justified by history ('We've always done it like that'), by success ('It worked OK last time'), by often legitimate reliance on the status quo ('If it ain't broke, don't fix it'), by unwritten convention ('We just don't do it like that around here'), by fear of the unknown ('Why take the risk of . . .?'). But behind every sacred cow lies an idea waiting to escape; behind every assumption is a golden opportunity to do things differently. If only . . . if only you can leap across the ultimate boundary, the boundary of your mind.

Whack Pack!

Challenge the rules

According to ancient prophecy, whoever could untie the 'Gordian Knot' was destined to become King of Asia. All who tried failed to solve this complicated puzzle. Then Alexander the Great had a turn. After fruitless attempts to find a starting point, he was stymied. Finally, he said 'I'll just have to make up my own knot-untying rules'. He pulled out his sword and sliced the knot in half. Asia was fated to him. Most advances have occurred when someone challenged the rules and tried a different approach.

What rules can you challenge?

One of the easiest ways of teasing out the unwritten rules is to ask the question 'What stops us from . . .?'. Despite the use of the word 'stop', this is by no means a negative question: rather, it is a powerful technique to define hidden boundaries, to identify the unstated assumptions, to trap those unseen sacred cows.

Let's return to the example of the sales-order processing system, and pursue Mike's idea of putting screens in our customers' purchasing departments. The key question is 'What stops us from putting screens on our customers' desks?', and ten minutes around a flipchart will generate issues such as:

- the customers will break our equipment
- the customers will send rubbish into our systems
- customers will have the opportunity to hack into our systems and see confidential information
- we can't afford to do it
- we're in the meat pie business, not computer engineers
- our mainframe doesn't have enough capacity to cope with a huge network
- we don't have any project managers of sufficient experience to deliver
- we have more urgent priorities
- the boss won't like it

and many more.

Each of these is a real issue and, in its own context, probably legitimate. But how many of them are real, fundamental, blockers? Surely each of these issues can, in principle, be unblocked and managed? Each of them identifies a boundary, an assumption, a rule. And each is subject to challenge. It is, of course, possible that on further analysis any one issue might indeed turn out to be a fundamental blocker – matters such as 'We can't afford it' can be very real indeed. But maybe there is a way around the barrier – even if, at first sight, it appeared to be insuperable. The process of identifying the blockers, followed by constructive challenge, is yet another means of spotting opportunities for innovation, yet another way of prospecting the boundaries.

Can you imagine how many sacred cows were sacrificed and how many rules were broken when the first supermarket was introduced? Or telephone-based insurance?

Learning from mistakes

While we are on the subject of rules, let's dwell for a moment on the subject of mistakes and failures. Often mistakes and failures are the consequence of negligence, accident or sheer bad management. Sometimes, however, mistakes and failures are outcomes that, for whatever reason, did not match our expectation. Is an unexpected outcome a 'mistake', or is it a consequence of the limits of our imagination? Mistakes which are unexpected outcomes may not be mistakes at all, but innovations in the bud.

The history of science is full of such 'mistakes'. The story of penicillin is doubtless familiar: countless people owe their lives to Alexander Fleming's recognition that the 'mistake' of an inadvertently contaminated biological preparation contained some then unknown agent that had 'erroneously' killed a culture of bacteria. More recently, the Russian scientist Boris Belousov discovered that a particular chemical mixture displayed the remarkable, and at that time unseen, property: most unexpectedly, and unlike any other chemical mixture known at that time, Belousov's chemical soup spontaneously changed colour in a regular rhythm over time. It was as if he had invented a chemical clock. The original paper describing his discovery was rejected by any number of reputable scientific journals, all claiming that his results were a 'mistake'. He had to wait over twenty years for his work to be recognized, for he had discovered the basis of natural rhythms such as the heart-beat and the stripes on the coats of animals such as zebras and tigers. How many scientific innovations have never happened because their origins were dismissed as 'mistakes'?

'Mistakes' happen in business too, probably the most familiar example being the yellow Post-it® Notes, that were invented as a result of the failure to discover a particular type of adhesive. A team at the company 3M were trying to find a formula for a strong adhesive, but their search kept 'failing' because the adhesive they had developed was too weak. But then they noticed that the adhesive was strong enough to attach paper to a variety of surfaces, including paper itself, but the weakness of the adhesive enabled the attachment to be peeled off without damaging the underlying surface. This property was not what they had been looking for, and, in the context of their expectations, was a 'mistake'. They could easily have dismissed the new adhesive as a 'failure' and continued their search elsewhere. Fortunately they didn't, and the yellow 'Post-it®' was born.

So, be alert to 'mistakes' and 'failures'. Yes, those attributable to negligence can be written off, but those that are 'mistakes' because they failed to meet our expectations are more likely to be indicators of the ultimate boundary – the boundary of our minds – where those expectations were formed. Unexpected outcomes could well be innovations waiting to happen. So make sure you don't miss tomorrow's penicillin or 'Post-it®'.

6 DELIBERATE INNOVATION

Training for innovation

Time for another 'Pause for thought' – an easy one this time!

PAUSE FOR THOUGHT

On a scrap of paper, make a quick sketch of a train – say, a locomotive and four carriages.

(Or, if you prefer, form a picture in your mind!)

When I run this exercise in my workshops, it usually gives one of three different results – probably depending on the age of the respondent! Some – nostalgics no doubt – draw a steam engine, pulling four coaches; others draw a diesel; very rarely, someone draws an electric locomotive complete with pantographs. We'll return to this topic shortly; in the meantime, let me introduce this section.

Brainstorming, benchmarking and exploring the boundaries are all techniques designed to help you get ideas and experiences on the table, and to guide you as to where to look for opportunities to innovate. We now turn to some tools and techniques for the systematic and deliberate generation of new ideas themselves – the act of innovation, the genesis of creativity. This chapter is the very core of this book, and what you are about to read may, at first sight, appear to be very strange. But do not despair, do not give up. When the penny drops, it will drop with such a resounding clatter that, all at once, you will experience how you can deliberately, systematically and safely discover new ideas.

Our starting point is a trip to Switzerland. You will recall from Chapter 3 the analogy between learning, and the carving out of valleys by drops of falling rain. Despite my personal obsession with things Scandinavian, a somewhat more intriguing landscape (from the falling raindrop point of view) than the border between Norway and Sweden is, of course, Switzerland. Within a very small area, quite close to the high-altitude ski resort of Andermatt, a raindrop might begin one of three very different journeys. One raindrop, falling a little to the west, might run into the headwaters of the River Rhône and then through Lake Geneva and into France and the Mediterranean; its neighbour, dropping just a shade to the east, will join the Rhine, arriving after its journey through Switzerland, Germany, France and the Netherlands in the North Sea. Yet another, to the south, will join the Ticino, and ultimately the Po, finally draining into the Adriatic.

But something else, something other than raindrops and rivers, goes down Swiss valleys. Trains. Switzerland has the most magnificent, and miraculously engineered, railway network.

Of the multitude of scenic lines, my favourite is the MOB – the Montreux Oberland Bernois. Starting at Montreux, the home of millionaires and jazzmen, the stylish sapphire blue and cream trains climb the steep slopes above Lake Geneva to Chamby where enthusiasts can alight for a trip on one of Switzerland's few remaining steam trains. Then the train climbs higher and higher until, after a long tunnel, it begins a slow descent through steeply wooded slopes. At Montbovon you can change trains to experience the delights of the 'Supertain du Chocolat' or even the 'Fondue Express' but, if you stay on, you follow the valley of the River Sarine, under the shadow of the crags of the Pays d'Enhaut, past the ski resort of Chateaux d'Oex and the villages of Rougemont and Saanen to arrive at the elegant town of Gstaad. After a sweeping left-hand bend under the fairy castle of the Gstaad Palace Hotel, the track climbs again to Schönreid and then reaches its highest altitude of 1275 metres above sea level. From there, the line follows the valley of the Little Simme river to the terminus at Zweisimmen.

Let's eavesdrop a meeting at the MOB head office, where Rudi, Max, Vreni and Arni are discussing the design for a new train.

> 'The Panoramic Express has been enormously successful,' said Rudi. 'Ever since its introduction, visitors have really enjoyed the spectacular views through the glass panels in the roof of each carriage.'
>
> 'Particularly along the valley of the Sarine,' added Vreni.
>
> 'So, it's about time we introduced a new design, isn't it?' said Arni. 'I wonder what we can learn from the design of the latest generation of high-speed trains elsewhere in Europe?'

'That's a good idea, Arni,' said Rudi, 'but we can hardly go at high speeds round our tracks!' he added, chuckling gently.

'That's for sure,' said Max, who had been chewing his pencil. 'I've been thinking. I wonder. Yes. Let me put it this way. What do you think would happen if our trains didn't have drivers?'

'Didn't have drivers?' challenged Vreni incredulously. 'That's crazy! You wonder what would happen? I'll tell you what would happen! Our trains would all crash! That's what would happen!'

'Vreni's probably right there,' added Rudi. 'I know that you can have driverless trains controlled by computers, but these tend to be on short routes – like monorails at airports, or highly controlled urban mass transit systems. But our track is too long for that. And the terrain is very complex – we have to have a driver to deal with events like fallen trees, animals straying on the line and all that. No computer could ever do that.'

'And if we did get a bad safety record,' continued Vreni, 'our tourist traffic would disappear overnight – people would lose confidence in us very quickly. I'll vote for drivers, please.'

'There is one thing, though,' said Arni, laughing. 'If we didn't have a driver, we could put all the tourists right at the front of the train. And they'd pay even more for that!'

'Now that's what I call a good idea,' enthused Vreni. 'How many times have you travelled in a plane and wished you could sit in the cockpit? Wouldn't it be fantastic for people to sit right in the front of our trains?'

'Yes. Wouldn't it?' mused Max. 'Why shouldn't they? Why couldn't we mount some sort of camera in the front of the train so that the driver gets a good view, but through the camera? Then the driver could sit anywhere.'

'You're right, Max,' said Rudi. 'You're right. Why should the driver take up the prime space in the train?'

'Suppose,' continued Max, 'suppose we put the engine, and the driver, in the middle of the train. On each side, we could have a couple of coaches and, at each end, we could have a fantastic panorama coach, with full glass at the front and the back. That way the train could work in both directions.'

'Fantastic!' said Vreni. 'What a great idea! But why does the driver have to sit in the middle with the engine? I'm sure that would work with a videocamera, but isn't there a more obvious place for the driver to sit? What about in a special cabin mounted at the front, but above where the passengers sit? That way the passengers could still have a superb view, the engine could still be in the middle, but we wouldn't have to rely on videocameras to enable the driver to see where the train is going – the driver would have just as good a view as the passengers!'

Figure 6.1 The Crystal Panoramic Express
Reproduced by kind permission of Groupe MOB, Montreux

Let me introduce you to a train called the Crystal Panoramic Express, which runs from Montreux to Zweisimmen and back. As you can see from the photograph, its design is unusual: the engine is in the middle, and passengers can sit right at the front, and at the back too, so that they all get a splendid view. There is a special cabin for the driver, in the roof, above the front passenger compartment as well as a similar driver's cabin over the back passenger compartment for when the train is travelling in the reverse direction.

Take another look at your drawing of a train. Where did you put the engine? At the front? Yes, of course. Why? Because that's where engines always are. Not quite always, I admit. Some old steam trains, because they could not turn round, used to push their trains from the back, with the driver leaning out to see the track ahead, and many modern high-speed trains have an engine at each end. But, when asked to draw a train, we all put the engine at the front. And where did you have the driver? In a cabin by the engine? Why? Because that's where train drivers always sit, isn't it? Is it? Is this yet another example of sacred cows, unwritten assumptions, more boundaries in our minds?

But wouldn't you agree that, yes, the design of the Crystal Panoramic Express really is fantastic? But there is nothing fundamentally new. There are carriages for the passengers, an engine and a driver, just like an ordinary train. And it still runs on wheels on a track, just like an ordinary train. What is different is the sequence of carriages and the engine, and the place where the driver sits. Yes, you've spotted it. It's back to patterns: as we saw in Chapter 3, innovation is all about recombining existing elements – the engine, the driver, the passengers – into new patterns. And here is another, very real, instance of a new pattern. An instance of true innovation.

But did you see how it happened?

PAUSE FOR THOUGHT

> **Read through the MOB story again, and look for how the innovation took place. Following the analogy of the raindrop, can you see the point at which the raindrop was hoisted out of its valley (the valley of the Sarine, no doubt, in this case)? And what happened as it tottered precariously on a ridge? And how did it finally tumble triumphantly into the valley of innovation?**

Provoking deliberate innovation

At the start of the MOB conversation, the raindrops are flowing down their normal, familiar valleys of experience, and the colleagues are talking of previous successes and the possibility of learning from others by benchmarking. The raindrop is dragged out of the valley when Max said, 'What do you think would happen if our trains didn't have drivers?'.

Now, at first, and probably second, sight, this is a patently stupid idea. But Max had chosen his words carefully. He didn't say, 'I think we should get rid of drivers', and he didn't say, 'My idea is that trains shouldn't have drivers'. What he did say was 'What do you think would happen if . . .?'. By using these words, Max was not telling his colleagues his answer; rather, he was inviting his colleagues to explore a particular situation, to examine the consequences of a hypothesis.

This provoked a reaction to what was perceived, not unnaturally, as a rather stupid concept, and a variety of objections were raised: for example, trains would crash and customers would desert them. But this was not an unduly harsh reaction, and the atmosphere remained lighthearted. It was here that the raindrop was teetering on the ridge.

It began to fall into the valley of innovation when Arni said, 'If we didn't have a driver, we could put all the tourists right at the front of the train.'

This is by no means a stupid idea, and it is a direct consequence of the absence of a driver sitting at the front. And, once the concept of putting the passengers in the front of the train has been tabled, it is but an easy step to think of somewhere else for the driver and the engine. And the raindrop tumbled down the valley of innovation. Tumbled twice, in fact. For the first suggestion was to have the driver at the centre of the train, with the engine, using a videocamera to see the way ahead. This then led to the suggestion that the driver didn't in fact have to sit with the engine, but could still be at the front of the train – but in the roof, so that the presence of the driver does not obscure the passengers' view. As we have seen many times already, while a problem is being solved, the current state of the answer (in this case, the suggestion that the driver should be in the middle of the train) is inevitably incomplete.

I have no idea whether my story is true. The Crystal Panoramic Express certainly exists, and its design is radically different from that of a conventional train. My story, hypothetical though it may be, illustrates how innovation can be stimulated by a deliberately provocative suggestion – a suggestion that is manifestly untrue, absurd or unexpected. In this case, the suggestion was that trains should not have drivers – a provocation indeed.

But the purpose of the provocation is not to suggest an answer, but to put us into an unexpected position from where a new answer might be seen. In terms of the raindrop metaphor, the provocation is the means by which the raindrop can be dragged out of its familiar valley and placed on a nearby ridge. The objective of this is not for the raindrop to stay, precariously balanced on a knife-edge, but rather to give us a different vantage point from which we might spot another valley.

And, in terms of the MOB story, this is exactly what happened. The provocation 'Imagine what would happen if a train did not have a driver' jerks us out of the valley of normal experience that, of course, trains have drivers. Many of the consequences of this provocation are indeed silly, impractical and dangerous. But that is not the point. The point is that the 'thought experiment' that trains might not have drivers provokes us to think about trains in a different way – in a way which is not totally conditioned by surging down the valleys of our normal experience. And by allowing this to happen for a while, from our unstable vantage point of the ridge, the idea that the absence of a driver therefore allows the space at the front of the train to be used for another purpose, such as the accommodation of passengers, is actually quite reasonable. From there, the rest is almost obvious.

There is, of course, no law saying that the only way to think of putting the engine of a train in the middle, and the driver in the roof above the passengers, is by the route I have described: there must be many other routes to that idea. Furthermore, after the event, the solution is 'obvious', as indeed were the solutions to the nine-dots puzzle discussed in the previous chapter. But what may be obvious with the hindsight of being able to look back up the valleys to the high pass from which you came, can be very far from obvious – if not totally out of sight – when you are at the very bottom of a different valley searching for a way out!

Provocations

The provocation 'Imagine what would happen if trains don't have drivers' is a deliberate mechanism to unlock our minds, to shake us out of our normal ways of thinking about an issue: ways that have been preprogrammed by experience, by learning and by success; ways that are conditioned by the natural flow of our mental raindrops down the valleys in our brain's internal landscape. By forcing the raindrop to the top of a ridge, and by giving us some time and space to look around, maybe we'll spot a new valley which had previously been hidden from view.

The idea of using goading, provocative questions as a stimulus to debate dates back to Antiquity: the Greek philosopher Plato was one of the most prolific exponents of the art, relentlessly stinging his audience into self-realization as a result of his persistent challenging questions. In more recent times, probably the most well-known advocate of using provocations as a spur to innovation is Edward de Bono, who has coined a somewhat ungainly word to capture the concept: in 'de Bono speak', the phrase 'Po: trains don't have drivers' is a code for 'As a mental provocation, let's consider what would happen if trains don't have drivers'. *Po* stands for 'provocative operation' and signals that the purpose of the statement that follows is not an idea in its own right but a bridge to somewhere else as yet unknown. It invites you to stand on the ridge and look around; it encourages the mental process of disaggregating familiar ideas to allow new patterns to form, just as we saw with our previous examples concerning literature, music and life. And it also embodies another concept with which we are already familiar, and now comfortable – the fact that, while a problem is being solved, the state of the answer is inevitably wrong. Provocations are not the answer to any problem; they are not a solution. Rather, they are mechanisms whereby a solution might be found not by chance, but by positioning our minds in a very particular place – on the boundaries of our normal experience. Using provocations is therefore not a random, arbitrary process like brainstorming can be. On the contrary, provocations are specific and targeted, for they are always relevant to the problem.

By their very nature provocations are unstable, odd and alarming. As, indeed, they must be in order to lift you out of your familiar valleys. But because they are unstable, odd and alarming, many people feel most uncomfortable when they first meet the concept, and even more so when they first try to use it. This is understandable since, most of the time, we are happy and indeed successful, flowing down those oh-so-familiar valleys of tried and tested experience. However, by the same token, these comfortable journeys prevent us from having innovative ideas when we need them. It is therefore absolutely reasonable that the only way to unlock our minds – to break out of those valleys – is by proposing something that is odd, unstable and alarming! The logic of such a non-logical act is compelling.

PAUSE FOR THOUGHT

Provocations introduced deliberately to spur innovation are indeed alarming. In Chapter 2, however, we met three examples of provocations which are more familiar, although I did not use the word 'provocation' at that time.

The first was the use of figures of speech such as simile and metaphor. A phrase such as 'like a bull in a china shop' clearly links very different valleys in our mental landscape, and provokes a rich mental image.

The second was dreaming – a state in which our mind runs freely from valley to valley, forming new patterns and rearrangements of thought.

And the third was humour – as we saw, humour almost invariably relies on linking together different valleys in a provocation that results in laughter.

Fundamentally, these are all examples of provocation, for all rely on unlocking our minds – on shifting our train of thought abruptly from one mental valley to another, thereby creating a new mental pattern. All therefore have their role in stimulating innovation and creativity, especially humour – I can always tell that my workshops and seminars are going well when there is laughter during the exercises.

Provoking provocations

You might well be thinking at this point, 'Well, that was a neat party trick, but it was a one-off. Thinking of provocations is probably even harder than thinking of innovative ideas in the first place!'.

This is an understandable attitude, but one that does not in fact hold true. Provocations are quite easy to formulate, as we shall see. As a starting point, try the next 'Pause for thought'.

PAUSE FOR THOUGHT

Think, quite quickly, of as many attributes of a train as you can – aim for a dozen or more items.

(If you have a pencil and a piece of paper to hand, you might wish to note them down.)

Another easy one. Everyone will have different lists, but a typical one might include:

- Trains have wheels.
- Trains run on tracks.
- Trains have engines.
- Trains carry people or goods from one place to another.
- The engine is at the front.
- Trains are controlled by signals.
- Trains stop at stations.
- To travel on a train, you must have a ticket.
- Trains run to timetables.
- Long-distance trains might have a restaurant car.
- Long-distance trains might have a sleeping car.
- Trains must be safe to travel on.
- Trains have drivers.
- Trains have conductors, ticket collectors and guards.
- Trains are reliable.
- Trains are fast.
- Trains have the right of way at crossings with roads.

No single individual's list will be exhaustive, nor will the points be universally true – we can all think of trains which are slow, for example.

Preparing a list like this is easy, because it encourages us to float down our valleys of familiar experience, cataloguing the well-known landscapes we observe on either side. If there is one problem to avoid in preparing such a list, it is overfamiliarity – did you, for example, list such obvious assumptions as 'trains have wheels' or 'trains stop at stations'? Also, be sure to explore as many different types of valley as you can: the valley of physical attributes ('trains are big long things with wheels' is, in this context, different from the valley of how trains are used ('trains carry passengers who have bought tickets'). For, once you have prepared this list of the familiar, you are now standing on threshold of innovation . . .

Negation

Look through your list and formulate a statement which captures the *opposite* of each of your assumptions. From my list, this exercise would result in such statements as:

- Trains don't have wheels.
- Trains don't run on tracks.
- Trains don't have engines.
- Trains don't carry people or goods from one place to another.

- The engine is not at the front.
- Trains are not controlled by signals.
- Trains don't stop at stations.
- To travel on a train, you must not have a ticket.
- Trains don't run to timetables.
- Long-distance trains might not have a restaurant car.
- Long-distance trains might not have a sleeping car.
- Trains must not be safe to travel on.
- Trains don't have drivers.
- Trains don't have conductors, ticket collectors or guards.
- Trains aren't reliable.
- Trains aren't fast.
- Trains don't have right of way at crossings with roads.

Each of these items is pretty silly – by definition, in fact, for each is the negation of something that we know is familiar and consequently sensible. By the same token, all these items are provocations, and who knows where any one might lead? Some might lead to a more fertile new valley than others, but you can't predict this in advance, nor is there any guarantee that any will lead to anywhere other than a barren wilderness. But if you don't start out, you'll never know. And, with a list such as this, you are not embarking on an aimless random walk; each provocation has an inherent theme which will stimulate your brain in different directions – each will take you to a different ridge, with a rather different view.

The provocation 'Passengers must not have tickets', for example, leads down avenues concerning payment systems, proof of purchase of a ticket, the issue of free tickets, the concept of transport as a public service, differential pricing policies for different sections of the community or at different times of day, and a host of similar issues. 'Long-distance trains might not have a restaurant car' stimulates thoughts about how hungry passengers might get food – for example by phoning ahead to the next station for a takeaway pizza or whatever (a service that can also be offered even if a train did have a restaurant car) or providing a shop where passengers could buy food (rather like the familiar buffet cars), leading to the idea of having all sorts of shops on trains. Why not? What better captive community than a trainload of people with time on their hands? Why not have 'entertainment' carriages that show videos, for example? In fact, now you come to think of it, isn't a trainload of people just sitting in carriages a very dull experience waiting for some entrepreneur to provide a whole range of engaging (and no doubt expensive!) distractions?

PAUSE FOR THOUGHT

Most people tackle the nine dots puzzle by experimentation – they pick up a pencil and start joining the dots.

Suppose, however, that you start *not* by joining the dots, but by identifying some of the assumptions, such as:

- **the diagram is a square**
- **straight lines begin and end at corners**
- **I have to use a pencil . . .**

Then, if you negate these assumptions:

- **the diagram is not a square**
- **straight lines don't begin and end at corners**
- **I don't have to use a pencil . . .**

you will see the solution with ease.

Distortion

Another way of formulating provocations is to distort something which is familiar: to make small things extremely large, or large things extremely small. Let's continue the railway theme and go this time to France where they are designing the first high-speed train.

'Let's try a different type of provocation,' said Bertrand. 'What about exploring what would happen if the wheels of our trains were absolutely colossal?'

'Mmm,' responded Françoise, 'Well, one thing that might happen would be that the trains would be very high off the ground. That might even leave space underneath at ground level. I wonder, could we put a narrow-gauge track between the existing rails and have local trains at ground level, with super-big express trains literally going over them?'

'That assumes, Françoise, that the carriages remain supported on top of the wheel axles as at present,' said Alain. 'Another way of doing things would be to suspend the carriages beneath the axles. That way, you could keep the carriages at the same height above the ground as they are now, but still have monster wheels.'

'We're all assuming that the wheels have to be under, or around, the carriages, aren't we?' remarked Françoise. 'If the wheels were really big, wouldn't it be easier to put the wheels not under the carriages, but in the gaps between them?'

'And if we did that,' said Alain, 'the coaches wouldn't be bearing down on the wheel axles so directly. We could even suspend the coaches to a greater or lesser degree from some kind of pillar. It would almost look like a train of telegraph poles, each resting on a wheel, with the carriages suspended from the telegraph lines.'

'But if we did that,' continued Bertrand, 'the carriages would be able to swing or tilt as the train went round bends.'

'And that,' said Françoise, 'would let the trains go round bends much, much faster. At present, the carriages are one rigid assembly with the wheels locked to the carriage body, and the whole lot has to be almost wrenched to go round bends. But if the wheels are not under the carriages, but between them, the whole structure is much more flexible, allowing the wheels to move almost independently of the carriages, which could tilt to allow them to take the bends much more smoothly.'

'Hang on a moment,' said Bertrand. 'We got into all that as a result of the provocation that the wheels were huge: because they were huge, they had to be between the carriages, not underneath them. But you don't have to have huge wheels between carriages – they can be just the ordinary size.'

'But having ordinary size wheels between carriages still gives the benefits of flexibility and faster, safer cornering,' continued Alain. 'Of course, we have to make sure that any tilting of the carriages is not so excessive as to cause discomfort to the passengers, but the idea of putting the wheels in a different place has got to be worth pursuing.'

'Why,' said Françoise, 'why haven't we thought of that before?'

Why indeed.

If ever you see the new cross-channel train, Eurostar, or the French high speed train, the TGV, take a look at the location of the wheels. As you can see in Figure 6.2, with the exception of the wheels underneath the engines at each end and the very first set of wheels adjacent to the engine, the

Figure 6.2 Eurostar – look at the position of the wheels between the coaches
Photograph by courtesy of Eurostar

remaining wheels are placed between the carriages, not under them. This design allows Eurostar and the TGV to take bends much faster, and much more safely, than the conventional design.

Take yet another look at your drawing of a train. Where are your carriage wheels? Underneath? Once again, it's all about patterns. Eurostar and the TGV still have wheels. They're just in a different place.

We can now see how a provocation, expressed as a distortion or an exaggeration, pushed our raindrop to the ridge of the specific question 'What different places are there for putting the wheels?' and then down into the sublime valley of yet another innovation.

Fantasy

A third way of formulating provocations is to imagine that the issue in question had been resolved in the most perfect way possible. So, continuing our theme of train travel, try the next 'Pause for thought'.

PAUSE FOR THOUGHT

Think about, or write down, about ten features that you would associate with the perfect train service.

My list is:

- Trains always leave on schedule.
- Trains always arrive on schedule.
- Trains always have sufficient seating capacity.
- Trains are always clean and comfortable.
- Trains have good catering.
- Trains have other services such as power points and telephones for business users, childminding services for children (and their harassed parents!), quiet areas, and noisy areas.
- Trains never have accidents.
- Trains interconnect efficiently with other transport services.
- Trains are fast.
- Trains are good value for money.

This is, of course, a fantasy wish-list, which immediately provokes a series of questions of the type 'What stops [whatever] from being achieved?'. As we have already seen, this is a powerful innovation-enhancing question, for it leads us to the fertile territory of challenging assumptions and chasing sacred cows. Also, as with all provocations, a concept, idea or suggestion does not need to be practical in its own right: the issue is not the immediate applicability of any particular idea, but rather where that idea might lead.

As an example, the idea that trains might offer additional services leads in a variety of directions, such as the provision of facilities for passengers waiting for trains, perhaps similar to those offered in airport executive lounges. Many railway lounges could learn a thing or two from the airlines, as the Eurostar service between London and Paris has recognized. Swiss National Railways (needless to say) already have a special 'family' carriage with a play area for children. Grouchy businessmen will avoid it like the plague, and rightly so; my two boys loved it, as did my wife and I, for we could sit and read in relative tranquillity but still keep an eye on the children. What about a gymnasium carriage on commuter trains? Many businesspeople might enjoy – and be willing to pay for – a 20-minute workout on their way home.

To leave and arrive on schedule is a worthy aspiration, but real life suggests that, even with the best will in the world, trains will sometimes be late – even in Switzerland. Why does this cause the passengers such aggravation? The inconvenience, for sure, but much anxiety is caused by losing connections or being unable to let others know that they have been delayed. The train company might not be able to guarantee arrival to the minute, but surely there is much more that could be done to provide passengers with facilities to tell their family, friends or colleagues that they have been delayed.

Describing the ideal – building a fantasy – is therefore another route in to formulating provocations.

Random words

The three techniques of provoking provocations described so far are increasingly abstract, and step further and further away from the original problem. Negation is the closest, for we generated the negations by listing attributes of the problem with which we are familiar and then negating them; distortions are a little further away, for they require stretching some element of the problem; fantasies are still further away, for a fantasy moves right away from a description of the problem, as we know it, towards a vision of the perfect solution.

Our fourth method of provoking provocations is even more remote. Let's imagine that we've been asked to come up with ideas for new ways of selling train tickets. With this at the back of your mind, try the next 'Pause for thought' – you'll probably need a paper and pencil for this one.

PAUSE FOR THOUGHT

Forget about trains.

Flip a coin.

If it comes up heads, write down as many words, ideas or concepts as you can (say, 20) associated with the word 'frog'; if the coin comes up tails, write down as many words, ideas or concepts as you can (again, say, 20) associated with the word 'banana'.

Don't agonize: this should be an 'off the top of your head' exercise and should take no more than a couple of minutes.

Whenever I run this exercise with groups, I am always amazed by the diversity of responses, so don't feel upset if your list is radically different from mine!

Frog

- green
- slimy
- ponds
- spawn
- frog legs
- food
- Kermit
- puppets
- leap
- tadpoles
- lily pads
- Amazon
- rivers
- boats
- sailing
- movement
- running
- throwing
- sport
- balls
- fields
- crops
- wheat
- Woody Allen
- films
- cinemas
- entertainment
- TV
- radio
- waves
- greets
- friendly

Banana

- yellow
- tasty
- monkeys
- slippery
- boomerang
- happy
- Latin America
- Banana republics
- corruption
- the military
- imperialism
- rainforests
- conservation
- colour
- noise
- insects
- snakes
- jungles
- islands
- sunshine
- beaches
- straw huts
- pretty girls
- Tahiti
- Gauguin
- modern art
- cubism
- shapes

The above exercise is one of free-form word association, from a particular starting point. Whenever I do it, I find it takes a little while for me to get going, but then the ideas come in floods from all sorts of different directions, as my mind follows particular threads. And each time I do it, the results are wildly different, even from the same triggers.

To return to our raindrop analogy, a raindrop was plopped arbitrarily at a particular point in your mind – as determined by the word 'frog' or 'banana' – and then allowed to run free. As the raindrop tumbles, you note down what you see, flowing down valleys of related concepts (running–throwing–sport), or occasionally leaping up to a different peak and then down a totally different valley (Tahiti–Gauguin–modern art) by associations that may be either reasonably intelligible or quite obscure.

Now try the next 'Pause for thought'.

PAUSE FOR THOUGHT

You will have noticed, in the last 'Pause for thought', that the word association with either 'frog' or 'banana' had nothing in particular to do with the problem of interest – that of generating ideas for new ways of selling train tickets. This 'Pause for thought' does, for what you are now invited to do is to scan the list you just compiled, combine it, if you wish, with whichever of my two lists is appropriate, and see if you can come up with any ideas for the ticket sales problem. Don't reject any ideas that look stupid, for they might be bridges to something else.

This exercise links the associations of either 'frog' or 'banana' with the ticket sales problem. In essence this is an enforced provocation in which the provocation is quite distant from the problem of interest. But you never know, there might be links. I'm sure you came up with several ideas; here are some of mine.

As stimulated by association with the word 'frog':

- Give tickets as promotions at sports events.
- Have tickets available for sale at outlets other than railway stations, for example, at supermarkets (this was triggered by the frog legs–food association). This in turn leads to many other ideas about locations for selling tickets – why, for example, should London underground tickets not be for sale at newspaper kiosks or whatever?

- The 'leap' concept leads to improving the way in which tickets can be used for connecting services, or services supplied by other means, such as local buses.
- Another association of the 'leap' idea relates to queues. How can queues best be minimized, particularly at peak times? Can the queue be leapt? For example, could there be incentives for people to buy their season tickets, say, at times other than the peak of the first Monday in every month (or whenever it may be).

And from 'banana':

- The 'boomerang' concept leads to thoughts about return travel, or multiple journeys. Would the sales of season tickets, for example, be increased if they were available for a chosen number of journeys, rather than for periods of time such as by the week or by the month? Or maybe two different types of season ticket might be made available for different prices: one type on a strict time basis for those who travel very regularly between the same destinations; the other on the basis of a number of journeys for those who travel often, but not necessarily five days a week every week.
- The 'modern art' concept leads to ideas about ticket design. Are they well designed and informative? Can their design be improved? Are there features that could be incorporated for people that are partially sighted?
- The 'pretty girls' concept leads to ideas about customer service at the point of sales, training and the like.
- The 'corruption' concept suggests issues to do with fraud, errors and controls over, for example, the handling of cash. How sure can we be that the value of tickets sold can be equated to the cash received?

I wouldn't claim any prizes for any of these ideas, but you never know where they might lead. The key point is this: what would have happened if you were given a blank sheet of paper and asked to come up with ideas about selling train tickets? In the absence of the provocation of the words 'frog' or 'banana', would you have generated more ideas or fewer? Most people, when confronted with a blank sheet of paper, write down one or two items and then become progressively more demoralized: it is virtually impossible for most of us to tackle such an unstructured problem without triggers. This form of provocation – the use of a random word such as 'frog' or 'banana' – acts as a two-stage trigger. First, we put the problem of interest to the back of our minds and concentrate on word and concept association with the chosen random word, generating as long a list of items as we can. Then we see if that list triggers any thoughts relevant to the actual problem. The page rarely remains blank.

Whack Pack!

Let your mind wander

Much of our thinking is associative: one idea makes you think of another, no matter how logical the connection. Use this ability to generate new ideas. Look at something and make associations based on whatever you can think of: function, location, size, shape, sound, personal, opposite, weird, and so on.

Example: work, play, actor, star, sun, light, bulb, tulips, kiss, love, tennis, net, profit, prophet, oracle, auricle, heart, life.

What things does your idea remind you of? What do each of these remind you of? How can you use this cluster of associations to develop your idea?

Reproduced, with permission, from *Creative Whack Pack*
©*Roger von Oech. Box 7354 Menlo Park, CA 94026 USA*

Would you like another try? See what happens next.

PAUSE FOR THOUGHT

You have been asked by a life assurance company to suggest some ideas for an advertising slogan. Use the random word 'ladder'.

How did you get on? And imagine how you would have fared had you been asked for ideas stone cold.

My list for ladder is:

Ladder

- length
- reach
- height
- rungs
- up
- crossing
- scaling
- climbing
- fire engine
- police car
- window
  cleaner

- steeplejack
- steeple
- church
- cleric
- squash
- sports
- vegetables
- food
- stairs
- steps

- Montmartre
- Rome
- Pope
- madder
- gladder
- sadder
- saddler
- horses
- animals

You can easily follow the trains of thought: a number of words associated with climbing and going up; people who climb, and related concepts; steeplejacks climb steeples that are on churches; then a change of tack to squash ladders, leading to sports; a squash is also a form of vegetable; stairs and steps also go up; Montmartre has a famous flight of steps, as does Rome, leading to Pope; then another change of tack, this time a linguistic one – words that rhyme with ladder; from sadder to saddler, and hence horses and animals. The list could go on and on and . . .

The next step. Does this list generate any ideas for an advertising slogan for a life assurance company? What about:

- For the summit of protection, assure your life with . . .
- Even steeplejacks assure their lives with . . .
- Don't be sad, be glad you're assured with . . .
- Our policies won't set your pocket on fire . . .
- Don't saddle yourself with outrageous premiums . . .
- See your savings escalate with . . .

Advertising agencies clearly have nothing to fear from me! But this list is at least six times longer than it might have been otherwise and, had I done the exercise with a small group of people, the chances are that something quite good would have emerged – as indeed it has when I have done this exercise with various clients.

How do you select a random word? Quite by chance – don't try to second-guess one or find one that fits the problem. Pick up a newspaper or book, turn to an arbitrary page, think of a three-digit number, use the first two digits to find a row of newsprint, and the third digit to count along the row to a word. Nouns tend to work best, so look for the nearest noun and use that.

CASE FILE

In my conferences and seminars, I often ask the delegates to devise an advertising slogan for an insurance company using the random word 'tennis'. Here are some of the slogans that were created in an exercise lasting just ten minutes:

- Don't get caught: use . . . (court!!)
- No backhanders with . . .
- You're a net winner with . . .
- No fault insurance with . . .
- You can't fault our service!

- Advantage . . . [company name]
- We're no racket
- 'Forty? Love . . . time to insure with . . .'
- Even rally drivers insure with . . .

Whack Pack!

Try a random idea

There was once an Indian medicine man who made hunting maps for his tribe. When game got sparse, he'd put a fresh piece of leather in the sun to dry. Then he'd fold and twist it, and then smooth it out. The rawhide was now etched with lines. He marked some reference points, and a new map was created. When the hunters followed the map's newly defined trails, they usually discovered abundant game. Moral: by letting the rawhide's random folds represent trails, he pointed the hunters to places they hadn't looked. Stimulate your thinking in a similar way. Pick a word at random: 'magnet'. How does it relate to what you're doing? What associations can you make?

Reproduced, with permission, from *Creative Whack Pack*
©*Roger von Oech. Box 7354 Menlo Park, CA 94026 USA*

Time to reflect

Let's now take stock of the last few chapters.

The central concepts are those met earlier in Part 1: the raindrop metaphor, in which innovation is likened to the need to take a raindrop out of the valleys of familiar experience on to the top of a ridge; the recognition that innovation is about the formation of new patterns from existing elements; the realization that those elements are our ideas and experiences; the willingness to have those ideas and experiences challenged and disaggregated before they can be reformed into new ideas.

All the tools and techniques we have met are designed to facilitate one or more of these processes.

We first explored some techniques for gathering ideas together. We saw that, although *brainstorming* can be fun, a totally unstructured approach risks leading us nowhere, albeit happily. *Benchmarking*, often perceived as a panacea, can be useful, but look out for problems of definition, and the legitimate desire of competitors to keep their processes, as opposed to their numbers, secret.

We then asked the question '*Where is the best place to look for opportunities for innovation?*', to which we answered, in general, '*At the boundaries*' – the boundaries of managerial responsibilities, organizations and the mind. Remember the nine dots? With a paint roller? You'll never forget that.

And so we came to the very heart of the matter. How, specifically, can you stimulate, deliberately and systematically, safely and consistently, new ideas? By using *provocations*, that's how. By deliberately suggesting something patently absurd and seeing what happens next. Yes, provocations are absurd – that is precisely why they work. Provocations are focused earthquakes in our mental landscapes that jolt those raindrops out of their accustomed valleys on to a neighbouring ridge. And, because the raindrops are precariously balanced on some ridge, we should expect provocations to be alarming, crazy or even stupid. But provocations are not ideas in their own right: they are steps towards new ideas; passes in our mental landscapes which allow those raindrops to migrate from the valleys of the known and familiar to those hidden valleys of innovation. Yes, provocations deny logic. Yes, provocations feel odd. But how else can you lift those raindrops out? So, when using provocations, let it be. Do not demand logic; do not seek practicality. Allow the provocations to flow where they will: provocations have value not by virtue of what they are, but by virtue of what they become.

Provocations are easy to formulate, and we explored four different ways of generating them:

- **Negation** – in which what is usually assumed to be a fundamental attribute of a concept is denied ('trains have no drivers').
- **Distortion** – in which the characteristics of a particular attribute of a concept are significantly distorted ('the wheels are huge').

- **Fantasy** – in which you imagine the best possible result ('what would the perfect train service look like?').
- **Random words** – in which the associations of a random word are explored to see what new ideas are triggered ('frog').

It takes a little while to become comfortable using provocations, and some people never can. Provocations drive control freaks absolutely nuts – they just cannot stand the ambiguity of that precarious intermediate state when those raindrops are not quite toppling over the edge. So have a good story ready when your control freak boss just happens to drop by when you are exploring the provocation that banks do not handle money. Logicians find provocations difficult too, for they are always searching for the reason why – the rational explanation. The paradox, of course, is that it is a logical necessity for the process of innovation to be non-logical: logic will inevitably drive you down the valleys of proven experience and away from innovation!

Yes, you can unlock your mind!

My best advice is for you to try it. Experiment with one or two of the techniques by yourself, and then try them in a small, safe group. Very soon, you will feel confident. And you will never be stuck for a new idea ever again. For the process works, it really does. If you follow the steps defined in the following box, you will be amazed at what will happen.

Deliberate innovation – the process

- Gather a small group – say 6 or 8 people.
- Define the problem you wish to address, ideally expressed in 'how to' terms: for example 'How can we influence our customers to buy more of our product?'.
- Individually, write down about ten assumptions you normally make about that issue: for example, the assumptions you make about customers, about their buying habits, about your products, about your ability (or inability!) to influence them.
- Share the assumptions around the group.
- Choose one assumption to negate, exaggerate, fantasize about, or otherwise challenge.
- Then see what happens.
- You will be amazed.

One startling aspect of this process is that identifying new ideas is, literally, the *last* thing you will do! This is surprising, for isn't the purpose of an innovation workshop to do just that? So shouldn't you start the workshop with a blank flipchart and brainstorm as many ideas as you can?

No.

Once a problem has been defined, the starting point is to define *what you know about the problem, not what you don't know.* By specifying the assumptions which you make about the problem, you are in essence mapping out the 'contours' of the mental 'landscape' – the shapes of the 'valleys' through which your 'raindrops' naturally fall. These assumptions therefore define the boundaries of the issue as you perceive them – the boundaries that you must break through if you are to innovate. And the first, and easiest, way of doing this is simply by sharing your assumptions with other people. Because we are all different, we will inevitably assume different things, and the question 'Wow, why did you assume that?' will inevitably lead to a new idea.

CASE FILE

The process really works – I have used it dozens of times to incredible effect, so let me relate just one anecdote drawn from a bank.

The problem the group agreed on was: 'how can we increase our prices, so increasing our margins, without driving business away?'

The first step was *not* to brainstorm ideas, but for everyone to write down their assumptions: assumptions about prices, about customers, about margins, about relationships. These were then shared, generating much debate about why individuals had assumed particular things, which in its own right was very valuable.

One assumption, however, was widely shared – that the pricing policy was strongly driven by the budgeting process. Having agreed a budget at an estimated volume, the prices were then fixed. And, particularly earlier on in the year, managers were very reluctant to deviate from the budgeted prices, just in case this might jeopardize achievement of the budget over the full year.

This then led to the provocation 'what if there were no budgets?'. Once people were over the shock of such a revolutionary provocation, this led to a wonderful discussion of the benefits of building long-term relationships rather then being forced to alleviate short-term pressures. This in turn led to a host of new ideas, all of which, of course, could operate even in the presence of a budget.

A further important feature of the process is for all the workshop participants to write down their own six or ten assumptions by themselves, without discussion. This forces everyone to think about the problem and enables everyone to contribute to the sharing session.

Once the assumptions have been shared, choose one assumption and construct a provocation, either by assuming the assumption no longer applies, exaggerating its effect, or fantasizing. Then let the discussion run free, and see what happens. I continue to be staggered at the quality and variety of the innovation that inevitably results. And the process is so simple!

No! Innovation is not about lightning strikes, about Einstein, about slavishly copying what someone else does, or about playing catch-up.

> To me, the answer's different, for to
> nurture innovation
> You must find a way to motivate, provoke
> the liberation
> Of the power of the people in the whole
> organization
> That means you, and me, and us – we all
> have great imagination!

Now you know why the rhyme says 'provoke'.

PAUSE FOR THOUGHT

WHAT IS THE KEY TO INNOVATION?

As the following piece of music illustrates, the key is F major!

The notes are significant.

They are C, E, G, B flat, C, A and F.

They stand for

C   Copy, benchmark and gather as many ideas as you can

E   Explore the boundaries, especially the boundaries of your mind

G   Generate, goad ideas by provocation

B flat   Be flat-structured, avoid hierarchies, and empower people to think

C   Challenge the rules

AF   Allow failure, and learn from mistakes

7 EVALUATION

Unfortunately, not all ideas are good ones

So, at last you've done it. You've had that great idea – an idea so good that everyone has said, 'That's so obvious, why haven't we thought of it before?'. Who knows why not? But what does that matter? The fact is that no-one *has* had that idea before, and now you have. Fantastic!

There's only one problem. There is no law saying that all new ideas are good ones. Even mine. And the history of business is full of ideas which seemed good at the time but just didn't work – for whatever reason – in practice. Remember the Ford Edsel? That car cost a fortune and was based on very comprehensive market research. But it failed. And then there was the promotion launched by a domestic appliance manufacturer: 'Buy one of our appliances and get a free transatlantic air ticket.' They miscalculated how many people would see this as a means of getting a cheap transatlantic air ticket and a gift of a free appliance.

So far, I have been weaving three parallel themes: the first has been concerned with the theoretical basis for innovation, and has taken us through the ideas relating to the importance of patterns, and the raindrop metaphor; the second has been about tools and techniques, such as provocations; and the third has been about interpersonal behaviours and the way in which innovation can be killed stone dead, or encouraged, depending on our organizational culture, our local subculture, and our personal style.

Within this third, behavioural, theme I have stressed time and again the importance of maintaining a positive, supportive atmosphere, of not putting people down, of not saying 'no', and of allowing seemingly crazy ideas to take their natural course as provocations.

There comes a time, however, when ideas must be evaluated, and the better ones separated from the weaker. Inevitably, this process has a negative side: some ideas get rejected. But even this negative act can be carried out in a constructive, businesslike and professional fashion, without leaving the author of the idea damaged, and without setting a precedent which guarantees that no-one will ever risk opening their mouths again. That is what this chapter is about.

Timing

One important aspect of evaluation concerns timing. Don't evaluate too soon. Too soon in this context means at any time before the idea is fully rounded, understood and thought through; any time before the author of the idea knows enough about it to defend it competently. Initially, ideas are too fragile to be able to defend themselves and, if they are killed off too soon, you will always wonder what would have happened if the idea had developed to full maturity. On the other hand, once an idea is robust and tangible, it can then hold its own and fight for survival fairly among other competing ideas.

Remember that while a problem is being solved, the current state of the solution is necessarily wrong; another way of putting this is in terms of the raindrop metaphor – while a raindrop teeters on a ridge between a known valley and a valley yet to be discovered, it is necessarily in a precarious and unstable position.

It is very easy to challenge ideas while the problem is being solved, whilst the raindrop is on the ridge, with the inevitable consequence of destroying the idea. So resist the temptation to score a quick political point by challenging too soon. Wait until the problem is solved and the idea can stand on its own two feet.

Some thoughts on evaluation

The key to sound, professional and commercially sensible evaluation is balance – making sure that the idea is seen holistically; making sure that there is a correct mix of data, opinion and insight; and also making sure, as far as is humanly possible, that issues of politics, power and patronage are in the background. But what needs to be balanced? Much has been written on this topic, as, for example, by Edward de Bono in *Six Thinking Hats* and *Six Action Shoes*. My purpose in this chapter is therefore to summarize what is now well accepted as best practice, along with some personal observations.

Let's start by being positive . . .

WHAT'S GOOD ABOUT THE IDEA?

No idea has value unless it does some good. An essential aspect of the evaluation is therefore the articulation and sharing of just what is good about the idea. This includes tangible benefits such as improvements to sales, reductions in cost, improvements in efficiency and the like, as well as benefits that are less easily quantified, such as improving the firm's image or competitive advantage, enhancing morale, improving internal communications or whatever. Understanding comprehensively the potential richness of the benefit package is crucial, for it is the achievement of these benefits that are the drivers behind the idea – the motivators that keep people going as they transform the idea from concept into reality and the future targets to be achieved.

WHAT PROBLEMS NEED TO BE SOLVED, AND WHAT NEEDS TO BE MANAGED, TO BRING THE IDEA INTO REALITY?

No idea, however, is perfect. Just as we need to understand what is good about a new idea, we also need a perceptive understanding of the problems that need to be solved to make the idea work in practice. No, this isn't a euphemism for all the reasons why the idea stinks. Rather, it is a recognition that the world is full of difficulties, and that any idea, however apparently perfect (especially to its author), will inevitably have downsides somewhere. Recognizing and understanding these potential problems is not an exercise in stockpiling ammunition for the day when you can enjoy shooting the new idea down; on the contrary, this list can help build consensus and guide you as to what needs to be managed to make the idea successful.

WHAT DATA DO WE NEED?

In business, the implementation of a new idea is likely to change something. The process of change will incur costs, and the future delivery of the benefits is likely to have some impact on something measurable: perhaps it is an increase in sales revenue attributable to a new product; perhaps it is an increase in productivity attributable to a new process; perhaps it is a change in people's attitudes, knowledge or behaviour. Sometimes these measurable effects are less obvious, but I would argue strongly that they are there if you look hard enough: indeed, if you are unable to envisage the difference the idea would make, how would you ever know whether or not its implementation was successful? And why would you ever bother to do it in the first place?

An idea is therefore best evaluated in the light of appropriate data, so that we all know what we are in for, we can assess costs and benefits as far as possible, we can agree on the vision of the future, and we can set targets for what we want to achieve.

This is not an argument, by the way, for conventional cost–benefit analysis. I am not advocating that new ideas should be evaluated only by comparing future benefits to future costs and accepting the idea if and only if the cost–benefit shows a 'surplus'. Cost–benefit analysis is fraught with difficulties such as:

- Costs are often within an organization's control, or can be made so by virtue of contract law. As a consequence, accountants can usually forecast costs tolerably well. Benefits, on the other hand, tend to depend on external circumstances (sales of a new product, for example), and any forecast is necessarily subject to considerable uncertainty. Skilled operators soon learn that the cost–benefit argument can be well fudged by pitching a sales line at the level of whatever hurdles have to be jumped. The test then becomes 'Is that level of sales really achievable?', to which any marketing director worth her salt will look you in the eye and say, 'Yes. Of course it is'.
- Boundaries, as well as being places to look for innovation, are places to treat with great care in any assessment of costs and benefits. Just where are the boundaries of the idea? If the new product takes off, this will enhance our firm's reputation, we will be invited to bid for new contracts, our credit rating will be improved, we'll win the Queen's Award, I'll get a knighthood. Where does it end?

Every time I walk past St Paul's Cathedral, I am glad that Sir Christopher Wren was not (as far as I know!) obliged to cost-justify it.

So the need for relevant data to support the evaluation of ideas is a more abstract notion: yes, I need estimates of cost; yes, it helps to have insight into the benefits; yes, there may be much other relevant data too (market research, staff surveys, whatever); no, a necessary condition for accepting the idea is not a positive net present value.

So far, I have probably described nothing too surprising: most people would not find an understanding of benefits, a recognition of problems to be overcome, all in the context of relevant data, particularly contentious.

But the next one might be . . .

HOW DO YOU FEEL ABOUT THE IDEA?

Benefits, yes; costs and problems, of course; data, that's obvious. But feelings? Business is supposed to be unemotional isn't it? We don't go around displaying our feelings in this organization!

Don't you?

You might not talk about them – indeed, many organizations have strict, and usually unwritten, taboos about expressing feelings – but you feel them nonetheless. And you act accordingly. If you don't like something, you will, sure as eggs is eggs, avoid it as far as you can; and if you can't, the fact that you don't like it will be evident in your behaviour, the things you say, the halfhearted support you give. Most change programmes peter out just because of the lack of managerial commitment – a euphemism for 'I don't like this' – which spreads like a contagious virus throughout the organization. On the other hand, if you do like something, you will advocate it, enthuse about it, generate energy around it – and, as a result, inspire those around you.

Another vital component of the evaluation process is therefore the articulation of emotion – of feelings. In safety. And in recognition of the very fundamental fact that emotions and feelings will make themselves evident, sooner or later, in many explicit and implicit ways. So it is far, far better to get them on the table now, rather than suffer the backlash later.

Questions such as:

- How do you feel about that?
- How do you think other people – staff, customers, colleagues, the community – will feel?

are allowed. As are answers like:

- I just don't like it. In my gut, I just don't.
- Great! Just great!
- I don't know. I need to think about it.
- I wonder? Maybe we should ask them (the staff, customers, whatever). What about a survey?

There is, however, one question which is *not* allowed.

- Why?

Let me put that in context:

> 'That's been a good discussion about the proposed appraisal process,' said Cathy, 'How do you feel about it, Nicholas?'
>
> 'Good,' he replied. 'I really think it will work.'
>
> 'Andrew?'

'Mmm. I'm not so sure. I need to think about it. I guess I don't really like it.'

'Why's that, Andrew?' enquired Pat.

'Well, er . . .'

How do you feel when you have expressed a feeling, and someone else asks you 'Why?'. I usually feel confused and challenged. Often, I don't know why I feel something; to me, my feelings are something I feel, and I don't require a logical audit trail of the 17 steps from here to there. I feel it, that's all – there is no logical explanation. So why is one being demanded?

Sometimes, though, I do have some explicit reasons underpinning how I feel, and maybe I don't want to talk about them: perhaps they reflect emotions I feel ashamed of, like jealousy, fear, anger and all the other things that happen within us all. Maybe I just need time to come to terms with a whole host of things.

So if I express a feeling, please do me the courtesy of not asking why I feel the way I do. Just let it be. Far, far better is to ask me about any problems I can see that need to be managed to make the idea work. That allows me to articulate any underlying fears in a much safer context.

The question 'How do you feel?' therefore sits alongside 'What's good about the idea?', 'What needs to be managed to make it work?' and 'What data do we need to help our evaluation?'.

The emphasis of the discussion of feelings so far has been towards the feelings of the decision-makers, often a small team of relatively senior people. It is very likely, however, that the idea being considered has ramifications far beyond this tight community, and so it is also essential to consider the feelings of others – of all those likely to be influenced. This, of course, is the arena of 'change management' – the design of a programme to ensure that those who are about to be subject to change can be helped and encouraged to understand it, to feel comfortable about it, to accept it, to adopt it, to enthuse about it.

Some people regard managing change as no more than a matter of giving orders, with the associated nuisance of training. Others take a different view and believe that the willingness of any individual subject to change is driven very much by that individual's feelings. They therefore seek to understand what different people think and feel as the proposed idea takes shape, is implemented and becomes real, and to design a programme of communication and training accordingly. And, in my experience, you can never start thinking about these issues too soon. So the question 'How do you feel about the idea?' should be addressed with the widest possible community in mind.

Managing the evaluation process

FOUR KEY ROLES

Think for a moment about a meeting you have recently attended where a new idea was suggested or discussed. Roughly, how much time did you spend discussing:

- the merits of the idea and the benefits it would bring?
- what was wrong with the idea and why it wouldn't work?
- what further information, if any, would be useful in order to evaluate the idea more fully?
- how people feel about the idea?
- other ideas?
- what should happen next?

In the light of previous discussion, which focused on the importance of the four questions 'What's good about the idea?', 'What needs to be managed?', 'What data would be helpful?', and 'How do people feel about the idea?', do you consider the balance of time appropriate?

Whenever I have asked this question during one of my courses, it is by no means unusual for people to state that, in their experience, almost the whole time is taken up with a debate on what is wrong with the idea and why it won't work. Often, this is adversarial, with the advocates of the idea being put in the witness box to defend the idea against opponents from every quarter. If the idea can withstand this trial by ordeal, then it will work; if not, too bad. Personal antipathies often loom large, and the opportunity for me to put you down by being destructive is too good to miss, especially as I am not obliged to offer creditable alternatives – a hatchet job is all that is needed. Political agendas, too, are often close to the surface, with alliances and behind-the-scenes deals: 'If you support me on this one, I'll support you on that one.' In one sense, this Darwinian process ensures the survival of the fittest, but whether the idea is accepted because it is intrinsically fit or as a result of strong political support is sometimes an open question.

Relatively little time is spent on what is good about the idea: people often feel this is unnecessary, and some organizational cultures have a taboo about recognizing other people's work – or indeed other people as individuals – as good. You rarely hear the words 'well done' in such organizations, except when said patronizingly.

Almost never do evaluation meetings discuss feelings, and the need for data is often merely a disguised attack: 'Do you realize how much this will cost?' is a question asked less in the spirit of an informed enquiry for relevant data than as a challenge implying that anyone who supports this crazy idea should apply now for a one-way ticket to the funny farm.

Yes, as usual, I'm exaggerating. But not too much. In organizations which are highly competitive, when jobs are only as secure as your patronage and your attributable-mistake-free record allow, then it is not hard to see how these pressures will influence the style of meetings held to evaluate ideas. However much you, as an individual, appreciate the relevance of the four questions:

- What is good about the idea?
- What needs to be managed to implement the idea successfully?
- What data do we need to support the evaluation process?
- How do people feel about the idea?

and the need to ensure that each is allocated sufficient time for a sensible discussion, we can all understand why meetings end up as they do.

But meetings don't have to end up as aggressive slanging matches. You can organize your meetings differently. To do this, you need the following two conditions to hold:

- You need a chairperson to allocate time appropriately, so that each individual is given space to air views, to test opinion and to summarize.
- The people attending the meeting need to share a common view of what the meeting is about, to recognize the importance of the four key questions, and to be prepared to behave appropriately.

The key to making this happen is to recognize that, in organizational life, people usually play roles rather than act as individuals. For example, you would expect the production director to defend the production view of the world and advocate its needs – that is his role. Given that role-playing is a natural part of the organizational game, might it be possible to organize a meeting so that the four fundamental evaluation questions:

- What is good about the idea?
- What needs to be managed to implement the idea successfully?
- What data do we need to support the evaluation process?
- How do people feel about the idea?

can safely be institutionalized by associating them with roles?

Yes, they can.

Take, for example, the first question, 'What is good about the idea?'. If a particular individual is assigned the organizational role of searching out all the good aspects of the idea in question, then it is organizationally safe to identify, and point out, the benefits – the bright side. And by playing this 'benefits' role, you are protected: you are expressing the role, not necessarily your personal opinions. Consequently, you do not risk being perceived as an advocate of an idea that might get rejected; you are not taking the chance that, behind closed doors, other people will start fantasizing about a new political alliance between you and the idea's champion. You are simply playing a role – a role that we all believe is necessary, and one that should be played professionally.

Similarly, there is a role for addressing the second question, 'What needs to be managed to implement the idea successfully?'. This role looks for the problems, the issues that need to be managed, the things that can go wrong. Once again, it is a necessary role and is one that doesn't have to be played negatively. By playing this role and separating the person from the idea and its associated problems, the identification of a problem is not presented as a personal attack on the idea's champion, but rather as an agreed recognition that problems exist that have to be managed.

The quest for data is led by a third role, on the basis that facts should have the characteristics of independence and neutrality. And so a statement such as 'In my role as guardian of relevant data, do we have enough information on the costs?' is a signal to everyone that this is a genuine search for appropriate data rather than a camouflage for the idea-assassin out to kill.

The fourth role maps on to the question 'How do people feel about the idea?' and is, of course, specifically concerned with feelings, emotions and the management of change. As with the other roles, this role affords protection, and this is particularly valuable when on the tricky territory of the emotions. Somehow, it is so much safer to say, 'In the context of the "change management" role, I have a funny feeling about this one.

Something tells me we're going to hit problems we haven't thought of yet' rather than a straight 'I don't like it'.

THE PROCESS

When evaluating an idea, the identification of explicit roles is both valuable and powerful. During the evaluation meeting, for example, the chairman might say 'Let's first examine the benefit package. I suggest that we all play the "benefits role". What are your views, Harry?'.

This statement institutionalizes a discussion focused specifically on identifying benefits. This makes it not only impolite and unprofessional to express a different, possibly negative, view, but also politically risky in that such behaviour would be explicitly, and publicly, contrary to mutual agreement.

A wise chairman will make sure that everyone around the table has a fair hearing and that no one is excluded. The only rule is that, during this stage of the meeting, you have to say something positive about a benefit, or express agreement with someone else's statement. Silence, particularly when invited to speak in person, is a difficult stance to take in such circumstances, for only the most curmudgeonly are unable to think of anything good about the idea or, at the very least, agree with someone else's view.

When this discussion has run its natural course, the chairman is in a good position to summarize and so help build consensus. If there is strong agreement, the summary can be along the lines of 'We all agree on the significance of the benefit package, and I can feel the enthusiasm around the room' or whatever; alternatively, if the chairman senses a much weaker consensus, a statement such as 'There doesn't seem to be a strong consensus right now on the scope and significance of the potential benefits. Joe, do you think it would be helpful to have more time to work them up?' suggests a safe close-down, offering the idea's champion (Joe, presumably) the chance to think the idea through more deeply, try to build a stronger consensus, or let the idea die with dignity.

To my mind, a discussion of benefits is the best way to begin the evaluation meeting, since it creates a positive atmosphere and, if the benefit package is attractive, stimulates a mood of expectation and energy. The next step is usually to discuss either problems to be managed or data requirements, depending on circumstances. Sometimes, during the discussion of benefits, various claims will be made about increased sales, enhanced productivity, improved morale or whatever, which may or may not be sensibly substantiated. If there is little factual evidence of the likely magnitude of a benefit, a natural transition from the discussion of benefits to that of data can be made by a statement such as 'We clearly agree that the primary benefit we seek from this idea is an improvement in the technical skills of our workforce (or whatever). What data would help to quantify this? Could we all now discuss this, and any other factual support that might be relevant?'. This immediately invites people to change roles and think about data. A number of avenues may be explored now: if background papers have been prepared, this may be an opportunity for their authors to present the results; sometimes relevant historical data, and an estimate of the anticipated future position is available, permitting the presentation of a 'before and expected after' case; sometimes the relevant data does not exist, and the meeting discusses what might need to be done, for example, by means of a special data collection exercise or survey.

Either after the discussion of data, or directly following the opening discussion of benefits, the meeting moves on to a discussion of the likely problems or, more positively, the things that need to be managed to bring the idea to a successful conclusion. When opening this discussion, I always prefer to ask the idea's prime advocates for their views first. There are a number of reasons for this.

First, it is very easy to fall in love with your own ideas and never experience anything other than total awe at how marvellous the idea intrinsically is, and how powerful the benefit package. Such rosy-coloured thinking is not only unrealistic and unprofessional, it can also be positively dangerous – especially when the advocates have power. So, as a matter of best practice, I believe that advocates should also play the role of critics, for this induces both balance and realism. Second, for an idea's prime champions to be publicly seen to recognize some of the idea's problems indicates to everyone else present that they are behaving realistically and are willing to take on board problems and issues. Third, the technique can prevent a potential slanging match for, quite often, an idea's champion is as perceptive at seeing the downsides as any critic, and it is far more powerful for the champion to identify some of the problems personally than to have all the problems tipped over him by others. Fourth, this self-analysis forces the idea's champion to recognize that there are problems and inevitably sows the seed that possibly these problems – and those that remain to be identified – are sufficiently difficult to overcome that maybe the idea is best rejected. This eases the process of rejection, should this take place.

Whack Pack!

Don't fall in love with ideas

If you fall in love with an idea, you won't see the merits of alternative approaches – and will probably miss an opportunity or two. One of life's greatest pleasures is letting go of a previously cherished idea. Then you're free to look for new ones.

What part of your idea are you in love with?

Kiss it goodbye!

Once again, the chairman should ensure that everyone present has a fair hearing, and should summarize accordingly. This may lead to a consensus view that the idea should be rejected; it may lead to a call for more data; it may result in an action plan to form task forces, or whatever, to investigate the problems further and define solutions.

By this stage in the meeting, there will have been a balanced discussion of the idea's benefits, the corresponding data needs and the problems to be solved. Often, this forms a natural bridge into the more difficult territory of feelings and emotions – usually by one of two routes.

One route is a consequence of the problems to be solved. Some of these will be technical (How can we modify the production plant? How can we build new systems?). Others may be primarily concerned with external matters such as the market (How can we test the concept? How can we fix the price?). Still others may be organizational (How do we retrain staff? What will be the impact on the current sales force?) or political (How will the Marketing Director react? What impact will this have on the balance of power between the centre and the operating divisions?).

As soon as we enter the organizational or political domain, we are inevitably involved with feelings and emotions. A question like 'What will be the impact on the current sales force?' is not very far from 'How will they feel?', leading to 'And how do we handle that?'. As already noted, a perceptive understanding of how people will feel and how they will react to a new idea is the heartland of the discipline now known as 'change management' – a whole industry focused on understanding the impact of change on people's feelings and behaviours, of anticipating and ameliorating resistance to change, of championing and sustaining change throughout the organization, of making change stick. The successful management of change is crucial if the change is to be long-lived; so often, valiant attempts at change are frittered away because of a failure to understand the enormous resistance that many people offer to change. This need not be active, hostile antipathy; very often, it is passive and politically neutral, driven by a lack of awareness of what the change might bring about, coupled with feelings such as 'This has nothing to do with me', 'It isn't my problem', 'Why wasn't I consulted?', 'If only they'd have asked me, I would have told them how to do it' or even 'If I stonewall long enough, this one will go away like all the others before it'. All of these are to do with feelings and emotions. So emotions and feelings are intrinsically bound up with new ideas, especially those concerned with process improvements or the introduction of new products or ways of doing business.

The feelings and emotions just described are those of other people. So the second route into this territory is for the chairman to say something like 'That was a good and constructive session – thank you, everyone, for your contributions. Well, we've examined the benefits of the proposed idea, the problems that we are going to have to manage, and we have a good understanding of the data requirements. Let's now talk about managing the change. Claire, what do you feel about that?' This is indeed direct, but not confrontational or overpersonal: it simply sets a new scene, allowing Claire to talk about what she feels. If she feels good, she will say so; if she feels less good, she will probably temper her response into something like 'I'm not sure right now, I need to think about it'. Remember to avoid the challenge 'Why?' – just let people take their own time. And, as before, make sure that everyone has the time and space to respond.

A discussion on feelings and emotions might open up a range of issues, from the need for further data (to find out how other people feel, why not carry out a survey?), to the identification of further benefits (people feeling good is a benefit), to the pinpointing of more problems to be managed (particularly on the organizational and political fronts). At the right moment, the chairman must intervene to stop everything being discussed yet again and to move matters further. Once again, an explicit identification of role helps this process along: an intervention by the chairman along the lines of, 'We've had a good discussion, but let me invoke my role as chairman . . .' signals to everyone that the chairman is seeking to halt the current discussion to summarize or move matters on.

So far, we have explored how the evaluation process might work in a meeting organized around the concept of explicit roles, in which the chairman has moved the session along in stages in which everyone sequentially discusses the idea's benefits, data requirements, problems and likely emotional implications. This is indeed one way of organizing such a meeting, but by no means the only one. One alternative is to invite individual participants to play a specific role throughout the meeting: 'In today's meeting, would you, Claire, please focus on the benefit package; you, Pat, the problems; Ann, would you please concentrate on data requirements; and Sam, the emotional side.' Those individuals then keep to those roles throughout the meeting. This can be a useful way of stimulating individuals to adopt different styles: habitual pessimists can be encouraged to shed some of their gloom by being asked to champion the benefits; incorrigible optimists can be forced to put at least a toe, if not an entire foot, on the ground by identifying problems; dreamers can soon learn that, yes, there is such a thing as data out there in the real world by playing the data role; and, even humanoids might just learn to appreciate that other people might have feelings – even if they themselves claim they don't by playing the change management role.

AND TWO MORE ROLES

We've already seen how the evaluation process benefits from the active participation of explicit roles representing benefits, problems, data and feelings but, as the process evolves, two further roles can also be very valuable: 'new ideas' and 'what next?'.

One new role continues the search for new ideas. You might well be thinking that, by this stage in the innovation process, there is no longer a need for further creativity: surely the purpose of the evaluation is to assess an idea that has already been well formulated? There is much truth to this and, in my experience, once an idea is in the evaluation stage, little benefit is to be gained by revisiting its core. Where the 'new idea' role pays real dividends is not in embellishing the core idea, but by generating ideas around other areas.

The most important of these concerns the problems identified in response to the question 'What needs to be managed to implement the idea successfully?'. This question, by design, is looking for problems, and it is professionally necessary for that search to be as thorough as possible: the more problems we identify in advance, the better our ability to devise strategies to cope with them. Compiling flipcharts full of problems, however, can sometimes be rather depressing. And this is where the 'new idea' role can really help. Whilst the 'problem identifiers' are compiling their list of problems, the 'new idea generators' are working on approaches and solutions. Yes, there certainly might be a problem with finding good enough staff for the new system project, but might it be possible to bring contractors in to some of the more junior, or less critical, roles on some of the existing projects, so releasing some of the best people for the new project team? Yes, there will be problems in merging the two departments, but leadership is the key. Who do we think is most capable of showing the required leadership?

You get the idea. Every problem has at least one solution, and the purpose of the 'new idea' role is to remain detached from the other roles, but continue to think of ways of solving problems. This keeps the energy and momentum going and stops the meeting from becoming overwhelmed by the enormity of it all.

Although the 'new idea' role is particularly beneficial in the context of identifying solutions to problems, it is by no means confined to this domain. New ideas can be very beneficial as part of the process of identifying benefits, of determining effective ways to gather data, and of suggesting ways to handle some of the emotional issues.

By virtue of the rather special nature of this role it may be preferable to have one or two people playing the role continuously throughout the meeting, while everyone else is possibly migrating from one role to another under the chairman's direction; occasionally, it might be useful for everyone to play the role together.

The final role is concerned with action, addressing the question 'What happens next?'.

It might be argued that the chairman should determine what happens next, and this may indeed be so. In my experience, however, I have often found it useful for a different person at the evaluation meeting to keep track of the 'to do' list, so that the chairman can concentrate on the process as a whole; can ensure that everyone has the opportunity to express their views; can help build consensus where there is one; can build bridges where possible; and can clarify divisions where not. The 'action' role is therefore to work closely with the chairman and, at the appropriate stages in the process, to ask, 'How, then, do we take matters forward?', to make appropriate suggestions, and to verify the resulting task lists. This role is naturally the meeting's minute-taker and post-meeting progress chaser.

How does the evaluation meeting end?

Don't expect an explicit yes–no decision after a single meeting: usually, after the first meeting, there is general agreement to carry out some further tasks – perhaps the establishment of some additional facts or the exploration of some problem areas to determine whether or not they are fundamental blockers. After one, or sometimes two, further meetings, a decision can be taken: perhaps to take the idea forward to a detailed feasibility study, or some higher authority as a business proposal; perhaps straight into the creation of a project team or task force for implementation. Alternatively, the idea might be rejected, the downsides having been judged to outweigh the benefits.

But, whatever the outcome, the process will have been fair, balanced and professional; no reputations will have been damaged; no good idea unjustly rejected.

Evaluating ideas

Remember, all ideas need evaluation, but

- Don't evaluate too soon.
- Remember the four key questions:
  - What is good about the idea?
  - What needs to be managed to implement the idea successfully?
  - What data do we need to support the evaluation process?
  - How do people feel about the idea?

Each of these corresponds to an organizational, and therefore legitimized, role:

- What is good about the idea? (*benefits*)
- What needs to be managed to implement the idea successfully? (*problems*)
- What data do we need to support the evaluation process? (*data*)
- How do people feel about the idea? (*change management*)

Playing a particular role is independent of your personal beliefs, and your degree of support or antipathy to the idea. Two further supporting roles are often helpful:

- What ideas would be useful, particularly as regards tackling the problems? (*new ideas*)
- What happens next? (*action*)

PART 3

TEAMWORK

We have to develop a sense of connectedness, a sense of working together as part of a system, where each part of the system is affected by the others, and where the whole is greater than the sum of its parts.

(Peter Senge, quoted by Rowan Gibson in *Rethinking the Future)*

8 OF ELEPHANTS AND WINE

What is teamwork?

One of my favourite films is *The Italian Job*, a 1968 comedy thriller starring a youthful Michael Caine. The plot centres on the robbery of a consignment of gold bullion from an armoured truck in the middle of the Italian city of Turin. The truck is immobilized in a colossal traffic jam, caused by the corruption of the computer program used to control Turin's traffic lights. The traffic jam also thwarts the endeavours of the local police to chase the getaway vehicles – three Mini Coopers coloured red, white and blue – the getaway vehicles escaping through alleys, along pavements, down flights of steps, over a weir and well away from the traffic-clogged roads.

The robbery is carried out by a team of 'experts', led by Michael Caine. Early on in the film, Michael Caine assembles his colleagues round a table and introduces them one by one.

'Now,' says Michael, 'this is a very difficult job, and the only way to get through it is for us all to work together as a team. And that means you do everything I say.'

PAUSE FOR THOUGHT

> **Think about Michael Caine's statement for a few moments. Is it a paradox? How is it possible to connect 'teamwork' with 'doing everything I say'?**

Teamwork, of course, is a truly sacred cow. It must feature in every organization's mission statement and list of values; it will also be seen as a checkbox on both recruitment interview notes and annual appraisal forms. No-one, except those who really don't want to be employed, or maybe applicants to be lighthouse-keepers, will say at an interview, 'No. I'm not a team player at all – I'm a real loner'.

But what actually is it? And how does it manifest itself? Does teamwork imply, on the part of the team player, a sacrifice of identity for the greater good of conformity? In business, does any random group of people, brought together for a particular purpose, constitute a 'team'? Does the team leader have the right to select team players, or is this implied right of exclusion itself a negation of 'teamwork'? Does the notion of 'team leader' itself conflict with the concept of 'team'? And, by virtue of my membership of one team, am I in essence in competition with members of another team, even though we work for the same organization?

These are not trivial questions; they underpin many of the stresses and conflicts of organizational life. The purpose of this third part of this book is to explore these issues, to offer some thoughts on what might be the fundamental underpinnings of teamwork and to explore some of the apparent paradoxes.

Why does this debate appear in a book on innovation?

As I have already mentioned, this book represents a continuous interweaving of three themes: the first concerns the theoretical basis of innovation, encapsulated in the raindrop-in-the-valley metaphor, as discussed in Part 1; the second focuses on the tools and techniques presented in Part 2; the third stresses the importance of interpersonal behaviours in either allowing innovation to take place or stopping it in its tracks. Since interpersonal behaviours are exhibited by the interactions of people in groups and in teams, I have chosen 'teamwork' to be the umbrella concept for this Part 3.

Our discussions will be far-reaching and might sometimes seem to stray far from the central theme. Also, the material is probably somewhat more demanding than the chapters you have read so far. I ask you, however, to be patient with this and follow the story as it unfolds. All, as they say in the crime detective novels, will be resolved in the end!

Our first apparent digression is to a somewhat alarming 'Pause for thought':

PAUSE FOR THOUGHT

What do you get if you cut an elephant in half?

And our second takes us back in time to ancient Greece, to overhear a conversation between Plato and Socrates, two directors of the Acropolis National Bank, who are relaxing in the shade of an olive tree after a hard day at the office . . .

Troubles at Acropolis National

'Evil's the wind that hard blows o'er our shining and rich wine-
   dark sea
Bringing distress and bad times to our bank, and to thee, and to
   me.
Markets have withered; our managers dithered; we've cut truly
   deep;
Plato, I'm lost, I'm so stressed and depressed; it's so bad I can't
   sleep!' said Socrates in melancholy tones.

'Socrates,' replied Plato testily, 'I know that you take great pride in the myth that you are descended from our greatest balladeer, Homer, but do you have to say everything in dactylic hexameters as if you are reciting from the *Iliad*?'

'I don't,' responded Socrates defensively, emphasizing the spondee.

'But you're right in concept,' continued Plato, 'this recession is certainly the worst we've ever experienced. To think that it all started with those cheap chariot imports from Crete. They've absolutely decimated the local Theban manufacture. It's a tragedy. And this is the first time that a recession has hit us so badly here in the south-east. It's affected all the service industries too – money-lending, insurance, even slavery! We've cut our costs just as far as we can and have saved every last drachma. What can we do now?'

'We had thought, of course, that our investment strategies would see us through. Do you remember, Socrates, the high hopes we had when we upgraded our central bead-frame, and then purchased all those personal abaci?'

'Well,' replied Socrates nodding, 'that was nothing compared to the disappointment we had when we provided all our insurance salesmen with those improved cleft sticks. They travelled more, and our premium income certainly went up – but so did the claims!'

'I was at a seminar at The Agora the other day,' mused Plato, rubbing his lightly bearded chin. 'The subject was this new-fangled idea of *Business Process Re-Philosophizing*. One of the speakers there was Demokritos – you know, the chap who's Head of Thinking at the Mid-Athens. Anyway, he was talking about his new, analytical approach: what you should do, he said, is break all of your processes down into their component parts and study them in great detail. He coined a new word, too – what was it now? Oh yes, "atom". That's it, "atom", meaning the smallest indivisible component part. He then said that if you study each "atomic" process, you can redesign each of the parts, put them all back together again, and, as a result, you will eliminate waste, inefficiency, errors and all those other things that plague us like locusts.'

Socrates looked blankly into space. 'Hmmm,' he hmmmed. 'I don't know . . . That atomic approach might be OK for some problems, but . . .' He lapsed into reverie.

A few moments later, he sat up, looked Plato directly in the eye, and said, 'Tell me, Plato. What do you get if you cut an elephant in half?'

'Eh?' responded Plato, somewhat startled.

'I said,' responded Socrates impatiently (he was never one to suffer fools gladly), 'what do you get if you cut an elephant in half?'

'Is that one of those elephant jokes our grandchildren are telling one another down at the Gymnasium?' queried Plato.

'Of course not! Tell me, Plato! What do you get?'

Plato knew Socrates of old. He was always asking rhetorical questions that he would never himself answer. So he decided to play along. 'I know what you don't get! You don't get two half elephants!'

'Precisely, my boy!' cheered Socrates. 'You took my point entirely! By cutting an elephant in half, you do not get two half elephants. What happens is that you transform a system which was working perfectly well – a living elephant – into two systems which don't work at all!'

'And,' continued Plato, 'that illustrates your worry with old Demokritos' atomic theory as the panacea to solve all business problems, doesn't it? Your elephant story makes the point that some problems just can't be addressed by the analytical, atomic approach. Some problems have to be addressed by seeing the whole picture: carving it up into smaller bits just destroys the problem you were trying to solve.'

'Indeed it does. Indeed. And are we wise enough,' asked Socrates, 'ever to see the whole elephant?'

Plato and Socrates were old friends and had no anxieties as they both once again lapsed into silence to pursue their own thoughts. Yes indeed. Acropolis National and its problems are very much like the elephant: an immense, interconnected organization with complex problems, linked together by the interactions of systems and people. Cause and effect are separated by both time and distance. What levers could they, as directors, pull to have the effects they wanted, without causing side-effects to backfire elsewhere? Yes, it is so tempting to analyse, to atomize, to split complex problems into seemingly simpler parts. But how can we see the whole?

The holistic view

Over the last few hundred years, the analytical, reductionist, atomic view of the world has met with great success. The key to solving problems has long been perceived as analysis, the paradigm being that the behaviour of a complex system is best understood by breaking the system into its component parts and then examining those parts in detail. This analytical view underpins much of current mathematics, physics, chemistry and engineering, and the technical world of today is a tribute to the genius of many minds who have analysed with consummate insight and skill. And it is a heritage that we have all been taught at school; not only have we learnt it, we all feel comfortable with it, for there is something very appealing about the notion that we can solve any problem, however complex, if only we can break it up into pieces small enough to fit our finite brains.

Despite the undoubted benefits offered by atomism as a means of tackling problems, the fact that this approach certainly works in some cases does not imply that it necessarily works in all, however much we would like it to. If the only tool you have is a hammer, as the saying goes, then you are obliged to treat everything as if it were a nail. If it is a nail, fine; if it isn't, you risk making something of a mess.

The anecdote of Plato, Socrates and the elephant draws attention to the existence of a class of problems for which the reductionist, analytical approach is not only futile, but fatal: the very act of analysis destroys the object of interest. Problems of this nature cannot be tackled by analysis; they must be tackled holistically.

PAUSE FOR THOUGHT

What problems have you come across in a business or social context which, like the elephant, cannot be atomized but need to be addressed as a whole?

Connectedness

One of the clues which helps identify problems that are destroyed by reductionist analysis is the concept of *connectedness* – the extent to which the interconnections between the parts are integral to the problem. If the component parts are only very loosely connected, then the process of analysis, which necessarily breaks the connections, does relatively little damage. The molecules of what scientists call an ideal gas, for example, are – by definition – totally independent and do not interact with each other at all, with the result that ideal gases can be described in full detail by reference to the aggregate, averaged, behaviour of the individual component parts.

But if the component parts of a system are very strongly connected, or connected in a variety of different ways, then reductionist analysis is very likely to fail because breaking the connections breaks the essence of the system. And the most complex, connected systems are those which contain people. People communicate with one another, people depend on one another and people influence one another in very complex and diverse ways. Indeed, the fundamental difference between the individual and any form of organization or society is this very connectedness – a connectedness that is central to all forms of human interaction, from a couple to a country, from a family to a firm, from a community to the Commonwealth. Chemists have any number of equations that predict the behaviour of an ideal gas but sociologists have no explanatory equations for the incidence of crime; astronomers can calculate the positions of the planets from now until doomsday but, despite valiant efforts, economists find it very difficult to forecast interest rates and currency exchange rates next week; natural scientists discover physical laws, while political scientists can do no more than observe politicians making human ones.

The analytical approach to problem-solving is necessarily doomed to failure when confronted by problems involving people. And if our current objective is to gain a richer understanding of one particular aspect of human interaction – teamwork – we need an approach which is necessarily different from conventional reductionist analysis. What could this be? Let us pause once more for thought:

PAUSE FOR THOUGHT

Imagine you are pouring some wine into a glass.

Why don't you habitually spill the wine all over the table?

And under what circumstances might this accident happen?

And so back to ancient Athens where, as the sun goes down, Plato and Socrates are continuing their discussion under the olive tree . . .

Who's in control?

Plato and Socrates sat in silence, watching the sun fall lower and lower in the western sky. After many minutes of thought, Socrates reached forward and poured a glass of sea-dark wine.

'Plato – how would you describe what I just did?' asked Socrates, with a sparkle in his aged eye.

'Well,' replied Plato, thinking for a moment just in case this was another of his friend's well-known trap-setting questions. 'You filled a glass.'

'Is that all? Would you like to say any more?' challenged Socrates.

Yes, that was a trap-setting question, thought Plato. I'd better be really careful with my next answer. Now I know that old Socrates here is a great exponent of free will. So let me formulate my reply accordingly.

'What you did, Socrates,' replied Plato, 'was to fill a glass. And throughout the entire exercise, you, Socrates, were in total control.'

'Hmmm,' reflected Socrates. 'And what, my dear Plato, what would you have observed if I had done the exact same thing, but with my eyes covered by a blindfold, and my ears plugged with cloth?'

'You would, of course, have spilled our good wine all over the table,' said Plato, laughing at the thought of his friend making such an uncharacteristic fool of himself. A blindfold! What will he think of next?

'Indeed,' said Socrates. 'Indeed I would have.'

He raised the glass, and looked intently at the richly coloured wine. Then, raising his eyebrows and leaning forward for added emphasis, he continued, 'Has it ever occurred to you, Plato, that your assertion that I was in full control of the level of the wine in the glass is only one half of the truth?'

'One half of the truth? What do you mean by that?'

'What I mean is this,' replied Socrates, not realizing that he was about to do something which was, for him, very rare – answer someone else's question. 'When I poured our good wine, I did not spill it – as I assuredly would have done had I been wearing a blindfold and earplugs – because, as I was pouring the wine into the glass, I was watching the level. Throughout the entire process, I was receiving information back from the glass through my eyes and ears, which caused me to control my pouring action. As the level of the wine approached the brim of the glass, I adjusted the position of my hand that was holding the wine flask so as to slow down the rate of flow until, finally, when the glass was about to become full, I stopped pouring.'

'So,' replied Plato thoughtfully, 'as you were pouring the wine, there was an interaction between the wine glass and you causing you to adjust your rate of pouring as the glass filled up. This, of course, implies that the rate at which you poured the wine was determined by the level of wine in the glass. And this in turn implies that you were not in control of the wine! The wine was in control of you!'

'Precisely!' exclaimed Socrates exultantly. 'Or rather, not at all! I was not in control of the wine, exclusively; nor was the wine, exclusively, in control of me. The two statements "*I am in control of the wine*" and "*the wine is in control of me*" are both valid, but incomplete; each is only a partial truth; neither is a full and accurate description of the system comprising me, the wine flask and the glass.'

'How would you describe what happened, then?' asked Plato.

'A good question, Plato, a very good question,' said Socrates. 'Let me describe the system. The system comprising me, the wine flask and the glass constitutes what I shall call a *feedback loop* – a system in which all the parts are connected to each other. My hand holds the flask; the position of my hand determines the rate of flow of the wine; as I watch the level of the wine in the glass, I control the position of my hand, which in turn controls the rate of flow of the wine, which in turn controls the position of my hand. Everything is connected to everything else – I, my brain, my hand, the flask, the wine, all interact together.'

'So,' said Plato slowly, as the understanding exploded in his mind, 'so when I said that you were in control of the wine, I was seeing only one part of a more complex picture.'

'Yes. That's right. Just the part you wanted to see,' replied Socrates. 'Few people would say that the wine was in control of me, however true that might be – and it certainly is as true as the statement you made.'

'Only part of the picture. Yes. I see. We're back to our elephants again, aren't we?' said Plato.

Socrates nodded wisely. 'Indeed we are. And when you see only a part of the picture, and you are trying to solve a problem, you stand every chance of coming up with a wrong, or at least only partial, answer. I wonder how many times we have done just that when trying to solve our problems at Acropolis National?'

They fell into contemplative silence again, each lost in his own thoughts. This time, it was Plato who broke the silence.

'You know, Socrates,' he said. 'You trigger some profound thoughts in my mind. Take for example our relationship with the world. When anyone makes a statement such as "*I am in control*", perhaps they are not in as much control as they might have liked to think. If all our actions are part of a larger whole, with ourselves acting on – and simultaneously being acted on by – the outside world, then we are all part of some very complex interconnected systems. And we can't hope to influence these systems – not with any wisdom, anyway – unless we understand them.'

'And by the same token,' added Socrates, 'how often do we externalize problems? How often do we blame the market, the competition, other firms' products, or just simply the other department or the other fellow? If the holistic systems view we have been discussing has any merit, then doesn't it follow that many problems might be as much our fault as the fault of that outside malign influence?'

'Rather than attributing blame,' suggested Plato, 'wouldn't it be better to recognize that all our actions are part of complex interconnected systems, in which our actions, and those of others, continuously interleave and intertwine?'

'This must be so,' affirmed Socrates. 'Yes. This must be so. But how are we to understand the complexities of such interlocking, interconnected systems? How can we see the whole elephant? It must be something to do with connectedness. Yes. Connectedness. That's the flaw in Demokritos' atomic theory, isn't it? Analysis necessarily breaks connections, but in complex interconnected systems, it's the connections that count. Yes. Yes. Of course. I wonder . . .'

Unfortunately, history doesn't tell us whether or not Plato and Socrates were able to solve the problems of Acropolis National but, a couple of thousand years later in Cambridge, Massachusetts . . .

PAUSE FOR THOUGHT

Once upon a time, three distraught businessmen could not stop spilling their wine glasses. In desperation, they each decided to ask a wise management consultant for advice.

The first consultant, famed for his prowess in cutting costs said, 'This problem is simple! All you need to do is to use a smaller wine bottle.' The first businessman took this sage advice and, for a while, the problem went away. But, sadly, he soon died of thirst.

The second consultant, renowned for his optimism and marketing skills said, 'This problem is trivial! All you need to do is use a bigger glass.' The businessman accepted this profound advice and, for a while, the problem went away. But, eventually, the glass overflowed once more, and, sadly, the consultant has long since cashed his cheque.

The third consultant said, 'This problem may not be what it appears. Perhaps if you take your blindfold off, you might be able to solve the problem for yourself.' This consultant was famed for his wisdom, for he knew that cause and effect are often separated both in distance and in time, and that it is far better to identify the cause than to tinker with the symptoms.

9 TAMING COMPLEXITY

System dynamics and systems thinking

If the conventional methods of analysis are inappropriate for handling complex problems in which the component parts are strongly interconnected, then either we have to leave such problems alone or we need a different technique.

During the 1950s, a professor at the Massachusetts Institute of Technology did not want to leave such problems alone: he wanted to develop a problem-solving approach in which inherent complexity does not get destroyed by atomism, but through which the problem can be made tractable to the finite, limited human mind. He was aware he was tackling a whole range of issues that had not been confronted before, but that had not stopped him in the past. His original training had been as an electrical engineer, and he had been one of the early pioneers of computing. A particular feather in his cap, of which he was rightly proud, was his role in the invention of what was known as 'core memory', the basis of a computer's main memory for about two decades until the introduction of silicon chips.

The professor, however, was no backroom boffin, for he had many other strings to his bow. As he looked out of his office window, towards the Charles River gently flowing through Cambridge to Boston, he knew that, across the United States of America, hundreds of millions of people were sleeping safe in their beds, despite the implied threats of the Cold War. For, during the 1950s, the United States had developed an air defence system controlled by the Strategic Air Command. From a command centre based in Omaha, in his home state of Nebraska, the US air force kept a fleet of nuclear bombers in the sky 24 hours a day, 365 days a year, to counter any threat. And he, Jay Forrester, had made a major contribution with the design of the SAGE system for strategic air defence.

But his attention was now turned towards complex, interconnected problems – problems of industrial development (Why do firms grow, and then sometimes decline?), problems of sociology (Does the provision of low-cost housing solve a problem or create one?), problems of politics

(What are the likely longer-term social consequences of increasing taxes on, say, property?). Although he was breaking new ground, he had some leads, such as the work of von Bertalanffy, Stafford Beer, and Norbert Wiener. And so, in 1961, Forrester published a book entitled *Industrial Dynamics* – a work that opened an entire new vista on how to tackle complex, interconnected problems.

His department at MIT soon attracted some very bright people, and the technique he had developed, called 'system dynamics', was applied to many types of problem from the behaviour of companies to the entire global ecosystem. The original ideas of 'system dynamics' evolved into the broader concept of 'systems thinking', as advocated in the bestselling business publication *The Fifth Discipline*, first published in 1990, by another MIT professor, Peter Senge. The use of the word 'system' in this context, by the way, has nothing to do with computers, computer systems or information technology: rather, it refers to the much broader systems concept as expressed by terms such as 'the economic system', 'the political system' and the like, all of which are complex, interconnected systems in which the interactions between people are integral to the system's behaviour.

Feedback loops

The fundamental principles of system dynamics and systems thinking are few:

- **Complex, interconnected systems are destroyed by attempting to break them down into their component parts. Accordingly, we must accept this, and try to bring simplicity, and therefore understanding, to bear in a different way.**
- **The key to understanding complexity, and especially connectedness, is by representing the system of interest as a series of interconnected 'feedback loops'.**

The concepts of feedback, and feedback loops, are particularly important, and if these are unfamiliar, it is worth examining them in more detail.

Our starting point is to return to Plato, Socrates and the wine glass. There are two intertwined themes here. One is the search for a comprehensive description of a (not so complex, but certainly interconnected) system comprising Socrates, the wine flask and the wine glass; the second is how we naturally describe what we see and ascribe causality (as exemplified by the statement 'you, Socrates, were in total control').

Our first attempt to describe the system went along the lines of 'Socrates is holding the flask; Socrates is pouring the wine; Socrates is in control'. Most people would describe the system in these terms; furthermore, most people would not only regard this as a complete and accurate description but would be quite startled if you were to suggest that it wasn't.

There are two features of this type of description that merit attention. First, this form of description is a *linear* view of the world: the system is perceived as starting with Socrates and ending with the wine being poured into the glass. Second, it is a statement of *causality*: Socrates' action of pouring the wine is seen as causing the wine to flow into the glass, and this is perceived as the only cause-and-effect relationship in the system.

This description of the system, and the causality behind it, is what (almost) everyone will identify, and, even if you ask, 'Is that a complete description of the system?', they will say, 'Of course it is'. If you don't believe me, try the next 'Pause for thought'.

PAUSE FOR THOUGHT

Next time you have a natural opportunity, for example, over a meal at home or with a colleague, pour a glass of wine, water or whatever and ask one of those around the table to describe what you just did. Did you get a 'linear' response along the lines of 'You poured the wine. Don't be silly'? And if you asked 'Was I in control of the wine?', did you get a response of the type, 'Of course you were. You really are being silly, aren't you? Has something funny happened at work today?'?

Not so silly, for you have just discovered how hard it is for us to identify feedback loops even when they are literally staring us in the face. If we find it so difficult to spot feedback loops over the dining table, how much more difficult is it for us to find them in business and society? We may not find it easy to see them, but they are certainly there, controlling us . . .

Socrates, however, had spotted the limitations of linear, myopic, cause-and-effect thinking. He therefore provoked Plato into looking at the system in a different way when he asked what would happen if he were to pour the wine wearing a blindfold and earplugs. Plato, of course, replies that the wine would be spilled, which Socrates explained in terms of the *feedback loop* which he had spotted but Plato hadn't: the loop completed by the feedback of information on the level of wine in the glass to Socrates' brain, primarily through his eyes but also, to a certain extent, by the gurgling detected by his ears – just as you can often tell how full your car's petrol tank is getting, even though you can't see inside the tank. And because his brain is connected to his arm, Socrates uses the fed-back information to control the position of his arm and hence make sure that he stops pouring the wine as the glass becomes full. The system of Socrates, his brain, the position of his arm, the flask, the glass, and the information concerning the instantaneous level in the glass, collectively constitute not a linear system but an interconnected feedback loop.

The existence of this feedback loop is self-evident and is used quite unconsciously. It is so unconscious, in fact, that we never notice it and find it quite startling when it is first described. Indeed, it is only when Plato is asked to imagine what would happen if Socrates puts on a blindfold – thereby breaking the feedback loop by interrupting the flow of information back from the glass to his brain – that the existence of the loop is noticed.

But there is another very important point here. Linear systems have a beginning and an end; feedback loops do not. They are continuous. Everything, sooner or later, is interconnected with everything else. And so, in a feedback loop, how can you accurately attribute causality? How can you say that A definitely causes B? In fact, you can't. In one part of the loop, A might indeed be the immediate cause of B; but as you follow the loop around, sooner or later, there will be some way in which B can be attributed as a cause of A. It may not be a direct causal relationship but it will be there, somewhere.

The dangers of taking a too simplistic view of causality were succinctly exemplified in our story about Socrates and the wine. Was Socrates in control of the level of the wine in the glass? Or was the level of the wine in the glass in control of Socrates? The answer, of course, is that each of these statements is only a partial truth, describing different parts of the feedback loop. But as soon as we see the entire feedback loop, we begin to appreciate that a statement such as 'Socrates is in control' or, more generally, 'A causes B' is only a very limited expression of the whole truth. At best we are not seeing our elephants for what they are; at worst, we are cutting them in half and therefore destroying them. What, then, does that say in general about our ability to influence and to control? How on earth can we do that if we are part of some huge spirals of interleaving feedback loops?

Feedback loops are everywhere

Absolutely everywhere – if only we could see them.

But, in fact, you do see them; you just don't notice them because they are so much a part of everyday life. At home, for example, what happens when you take a shower? How do you adjust the temperature? You first turn on the shower, and then test the water temperature with your hand (or perhaps your foot!). If the water is too cool or too hot, you adjust the temperature regulator up or down. When it's right, you jump in.

This is, of course, a feedback loop exactly like the one Socrates explained: in the shower, information on the temperature of the water is fed back through the skin on your hand, and you adjust the regulator to obtain the required temperature; in the wine story, information on the level of the wine in the glass is fed back through Socrates' eyes, causing him to adjust the position of his hand so as to control the rate at which he poured the wine.

It can be a quite different story when you are using an unfamiliar shower – for example, in a hotel. Have you ever switched on such a shower, waited a few moments and then decided it is far too cold? You then turn the regulator up, wait a few more moments, test the water again and feel it is still too cold. You turn the regulator up even further, test the water a third time and yelp with pain as the scalding water burns the back of your hand. At this point you realize that the regulator is now behind a curtain of lethally hot water and the only way to reach it to turn it down is by wrapping a towel around your hand. This you do, and, hoping you can grip the regulator sufficiently, you grit your teeth to face the ordeal by scalding again and thump the regulator in the opposite direction. After a few minutes, the water now runs Arctic cold, and the sequence continues until you get it right or decide to take a bath instead.

This too is a feedback loop but with an additional special feature. In this example, there is a time delay between the action you take (adjusting the regulator) and the effect you wish to achieve (changing the temperature of the water): in this case, the immediate cause (the position of the regulator) and the resulting effect (the actual water temperature) are separated in time. If you are not expecting this time delay or fail to assess its duration correctly, the natural behaviour is to interfere, and adjust the regulator even further. This, of course, aggravates the situation, and the water becomes even hotter. You then overcompensate the other way, making it icy cold again, and so the system oscillates between hot and cold as you learn to adjust the regulator more sensitively. At home, of course, you know where to set the regulator to get just the temperature you like and you know how long it takes for the water to come through, so you get it right first time; in a hotel, you don't know, and so you go through this all-too-familiar trial-and-error process.

But this oscillatory behaviour is nothing more nor less than the natural behaviour pattern of a feedback loop with a time lag. An unfamiliar shower is one example, but there are many, many others, particularly in business and economics: does the boom and bust cycle of many markets now have a familiar ring?

Another example – this one from daily life.

You've had a hard day at work, and you travel home in an irritable mood. On the crowded train, you think how lovely it will be to arrive home into the loving arms of your wife, who will comfort you by stroking your brow, giving you a nice drink and a gentle kiss. In fact, when you arrive home, your wife has also had a bad day, and she has been dreaming of exactly the same loving care and attention from you. But you just haven't got the energy. It's all been too much. So you slouch into a chair in silence, wondering why you are not being fussed over. And she does exactly the same thing. You sit there glowering at each other, wanting the other to make the first move, but without the energy to do so yourself.

And then you brood. Why isn't she fussing over me? I've had a hard day at work, and all she can do is sit there reading the paper. You get progressively irritable and even more stubbornly resolved not to make the first move. Simultaneously, of course, your wife is doing exactly the same thing.

Feedback loops again – one each, this time, operating together in perfect synchrony.

One way of describing the loop in which both members of the couple find themselves is illustrated in Figure 9.1. The diagram may be interpreted by starting at the top: you arrive home irritable. This causes you to desire attention and, feeling somewhat sorry for yourself, this makes you selfish and unwilling to give attention. Since your wife is wanting the attention you will not give, for she is experiencing exactly the same emotions, she retreats into her own shell and you feel rejected. This makes you even more irritable, and the loop spins off on another turn . . .

Some feedback loops can have pretty nasty consequences.

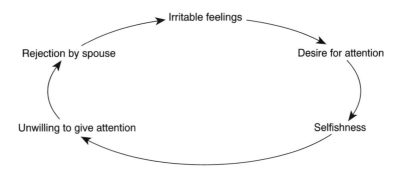

Figure 9.1 Irritable behaviour

This example, by the way, shows that describing events in terms of feedback loops is by no means limited to physical things like wine glasses or the temperature of your shower water: as we shall see, representing real life in terms of feedback loops is an immensely powerful way of capturing all sorts of different concepts.

Another example, this time from the business world.

Oh dear. Your star employee has just given you the bad news that she is resigning to join a competitor. But during the 'I'm off' discussion, she drops a not very subtle hint that her new package is not substantially greater than her current one, and she has always enjoyed working with you really. Losing your key employee would cause considerable pain, so you phone your boss, explain the situation and point out all the reasons why it would be a good idea to bring forward her next salary review by only a couple of months or so. Your boss, who has plenty of other things on her plate, agrees, and you call your soon to be ex-employee in for another chat. Hooray! Wonder of wonders! It worked. She withdraws her resignation! A triumph!

And when you get home that night, you are not at all irritable, as your wife soon realizes.

The next day, bliss! What a good manager you are! Didn't you handle that situation well?

But the next day, there's a knock on your office door. It's another employee. 'How come Jo's got that special deal? It's not fair, you know. The headhunters called me up too, and I'll be out of here like a shot as soon as I can. . . . Unless, that is . . .'.

Oh dear . . .

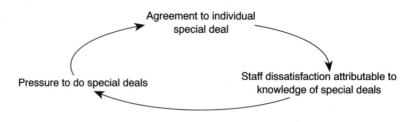

Figure 9.2   Risk of losing good staff

A feedback loop strikes again. This one can be represented by Figure 9.2.
This loop starts with the problem of the star employee's resignation – a
bad situation, for you don't want her to go. You want to solve the problem
quickly, and you decide that offering the employee more money will do
the trick. Under pressure to fix the problem, you agree a special deal.
What you didn't anticipate, however, was that news of the special deal
would leak out to the other employees – you had been hoping that the
deal would remain a secret. But, as soon as the other employees find out,
your quick-fix solution to the original problem backfires, with the result
that the original problem becomes much worse . . .

These three examples illustrate a number of points. First, they emphasize
that feedback loops are everywhere and are so familiar that we hardly ever
notice them. However, once you know what you are looking for, they are
very easy to spot. Second, they show the utility of expressing the structure
of feedback loops in terms of diagrams showing the major components
linked by arrows. Any two linked items have an immediate cause-and-
effect relationship, and the diagram as a whole represents the entire
structure. Diagrams such as these are called *causal loop diagrams* or
influence diagrams, and we shall meet many over the next few chapters.
Third, the examples show that feedback loops can be used to represent
many different concepts and situations, from the tangible (the example of
the shower) to the abstract (take another look at Figures 9.1 and 9.2, and
you will see that the ideas captured there are very generalized). This
versatility implies that the language of feedback loops, and their expression
in terms of causal loop diagrams, can be applied to many different issues.

The fourth point, the ubiquity of feedback loops and their intrinsically
looped structure, makes logical sense. As you will recall, our original
problem was to devise a method of representing complex, interconnected

systems in which all the component parts interact with one another. This connectedness implies that the very act of breaking the problem down into its component parts destroys the essence of the original problem, and that the problem should therefore be studied in its entirety – holistically. Does it not then follow that loops are a natural way of representing such problems? A loop is a loop by virtue of its connectedness: as soon as a loop is broken, it is no longer a loop in which everything is connected to everything else, but a linear sequence with a beginning and an end. Even a very small break in a loop destroys it. It is therefore no surprise that networks of interconnected loops are likely to be the most appropriate representation of complex, interconnected problems. Instead of deconstructing the problem to study the component parts in isolation, the exploration of feedback loops allows us to see what the component parts are, and examine their intrinsic connectedness.

How to draw causal loop diagrams

Causal loop diagrams often appear to be extremely simple, but they are sometimes quite difficult to compile. A good causal loop diagram is a succinct representation of the problem of interest, which quickly and easily communicates the essence of the issue, often to the extent that an observer might say 'What's the fuss? That's obvious!'; by contrast, a weaker diagram is cluttered, difficult to assimilate and prevents the observer from seeing the wood for the trees.

Some particularly perceptive people can construct highly effective causal loop diagrams almost intuitively: one moment they are talking about an issue, the next moment, there is the diagram. I can't do that: I have to compile them step-by-step.

As an example, suppose we are investigating how to improve the motivation of staff in a service business such as an advertising agency or a professional firm. Our central concept, our starting point, is therefore 'staff motivation'. I then ask the question 'What are the drivers of staff motivation?' and list them – for example:

- recognition
- job satisfaction
- salary
- fringe benefits
- fear of redundancy
- prospects of promotion
- freedom of action, and so on.

This list is set down only in the order in which they entered my head, and so the next question is 'What is their relative importance?'. This is often not an easy question to answer, and different people will have different views, but let's suppose that the ranking, from most important to least, is:

- salary
- fringe benefits
- recognition
- fear of redundancy
- job satisfaction
- freedom of action
- prospects of promotion.

This stage clearly involves judgement, and is heavily dependent on personal preferences – a point to which we will return at some length shortly. But having compiled the list in a preferred order of importance, the next question is sometimes even tougher still: 'In the context of the current problem, would anything really important be lost if we ignored all these items except the first?'. This question is designed to force you to look at the wood rather than the trees and challenge the items themselves: for example, is it really relevant to distinguish between 'salary' and 'fringe benefits'? Aren't these two items better treated as the single concept 'package'? Similarly, are 'recognition', 'job satisfaction' and 'freedom of action' that different? Is there a concept, such as 'personal growth', that encapsulates all these? And perhaps 'prospects of promotion' and 'fear of redundancy' might be two manifestations of the broader concept 'career prospects'. Now that this process of distillation has both clarified our thinking and eliminated clutter, our original list has now boiled down to just three items:

- package
- personal growth
- career prospects.

For the moment, let's suppose that we feel we can ignore 'personal growth' and 'career prospects' and that, despite the potential importance of these items, it is the 'package' which is the most significant. This then tells us that the immediate causality of 'motivation' is 'package', which we then draw as shown in Figure 9.3.

Figure 9.3 A representation that 'motivation' is most immediately driven by 'package'

The direction of the arrow shows the direction of immediate causality: it is the package which is

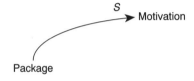

Figure 9.4 The symbol '*S*' indicates that as the 'package' increases, 'motivation' also increases: both variables move in the *same* direction

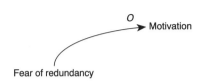

Figure 9.5 The symbol '*O*' indicates that as the 'fear of redundancy' increases, 'motivation' *de*creases: this time the two variables move in *opposite* directions

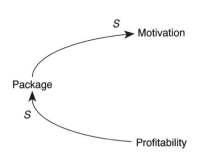

Figure 9.6 Extending the chain of causality by one more link . . .

perceived as the immediate driver of motivation rather than the other way around. But how does this influence manifest itself? In particular, if the package were to increase, would motivation increase or decrease? Our intuition tells us that, if the package improves, we expect the motivation to improve too. Since these two items move in the same direction, we conventionally write an '*S*' (for 'same') by the head of the arrow, as in Figure 9.4.

Sometimes, two linked items in a causal loop diagram do not move in the same direction, but in opposite directions. Suppose, for example, we had judged that 'fear of redundancy' was the major driver of 'motivation'. In this case, as fear *in*creases, we would expect motivation to *de*crease. This type of relationship, in which the items move in opposite directions, is indicated by an '*O*' (for 'opposite'), as in Figure 9.5.

Returning now to Figure 9.4, and having established that 'package' is the main driver of 'motivation', we then go through a similar process again, but this time with reference to the item 'package'. What are the drivers of 'package'? What is their relative importance? Can this long list be rearranged, consolidated or simplified? You might like to think this through for yourself; for the purposes of this example, however, let's suppose that we agree on the not unreasonable conclusion that the key determinant of the 'package' is the overall performance or profitability of the business (Figure 9.6).

Once again, there is an *S* linking 'profitability' to 'package', in recognition of the organization's policy that, as profitability increases so does the remuneration package.

And so we do the same thing yet again, this time focusing on profitability. What drives profitability? How are these items ranked? Can they be simplified? Suppose that the result of this is the single item 'sales', giving (Figure 9.7):

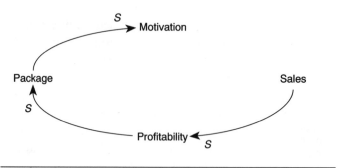

Figure 9.7 And another . . .

Are you happy with the last *S*?

And, surprise, surprise, we do the same again with 'sales'. What are its key drivers? How are they ranked? Once again, you might like to note down some of your own thoughts, but remember that this example was set in the context of a service industry such as an advertising agency or a professional firm. This kind of organization, of course, is heavily dependent on its staff, and much of the revenue stream is attributable to the professionalism, expertise and energy of its people. Maybe motivation itself is the key driver of sales . . .

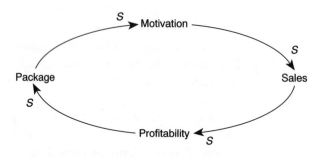

Figure 9.8 And another, until the feedback loop is completed

Well, well! The feedback loop has closed back on itself.

So, there in action was an example of how to construct a feedback loop. The process is quite straighforward and systematic, and one of the keys is to work *backwards*: having identified 'Motivation' as the central concept, we stepped back from item to item, asking the questions.

- **What are the key drivers of . . .?**
- **What is their ranking?**

- **Can these items be consolidated, restructured or otherwise simplified?**

And, usually sooner rather than later, the loop closes. They always do.

This method of compiling causal loop diagrams – working backwards – is particularly powerful when you are exploring how to achieve a defined objective, such as profit growth. If, however, you wish to examine the possible impact of policy decisions, it is usually easier to build the diagram by working forwards from the policy proposition. As an example, suppose you are considering a policy of cost-cutting and wish to ensure that the policy is fully thought through. The starting point here is to express the policy in terms of a variable such as 'pressure on costs' and then ask the question 'What are the consequences?'. This in turn might result in an increase in the 'pressure to compromise quality', leading to an increase in 'customer complaints', thereby increasing the 'pressure on profitability', feeding back to increase the 'pressure on costs', as shown in Figure 9.9.

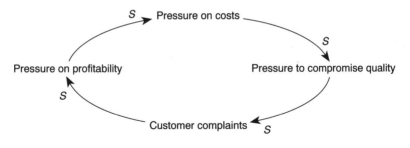

Figure 9.9 A causal loop diagram compiled by working forwards from a policy proposition

This is clearly bad news, and, to some extent, obvious. But we have all seen countless examples of policy decisions that backfire because they have not been well thought-through. By compiling a causal loop diagram of the possible consequences of a proposed policy decision, not only can you ensure that the management team has a balanced and shared understanding of the problem, and hence a genuine commitment to the solution, but you can also create the conditions under which fundamentally important questions such as 'How can we cut costs but protect quality?' get raised and discussed.

Two other tips:

- Try to use nouns or noun phrases as the items in the diagram – avoid verbs.
- Resist the temptation to include directionality in the items in the diagram: so, for example, use 'motivation' rather than 'increase in motivation'. Directionality should be incorporated by the use of *S* or *O* by the arrow heads.

One further point. Causal loop diagrams are inevitably simplifications, but this does not imply that they are trivializations: a good causal loop diagram is immediately recognized as offering a perceptive view of the wood, not the trees. To achieve this, certain items must be ignored, as we saw in the process of compiling the loop finally shown in Figure 9.8. This process of selection might be based on data or evidence, but very often it is judgemental or based on opinion. And sometimes, it is very difficult to boil immediate causality down to just a single item. In which case, no matter: incorporate two or even three items into your diagram, and trace each back independently. The diagram of Figure 9.10, for example, is just as plausible as Figure 9.8.

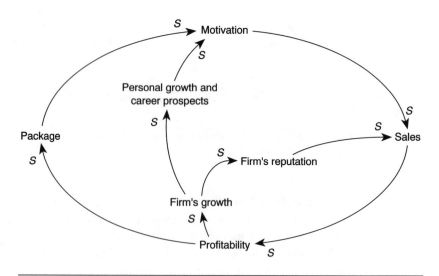

Figure 9.10 An alternative view

As you can see, matters soon become complicated, simply because we are trying to get a grip on complexity. The trick is to avoid unhelpful clutter, so always try to keep your causal loop diagrams as simple as possible, and add complexity slowly and carefully.

PAUSE FOR THOUGHT

Here is an opportunity to think about – or, better still, draw – a causal loop diagram of your own.

Imagine that you are the managing director of a chain of retail stores. Intuitively, you recognize the causal link between the overall level of sales and the corresponding profits as expressed by a linkage such as:

Your knowledge of systems thinking tells you that this statement, although true, is only a partial truth. Draw your own feedback loop, capturing your view of a more complete truth.

10 MENTAL MODELS

A nice problem to have . . .

'Thank you all for giving up your time this afternoon for this session,' said Keith, opening the meeting, 'but I thought it would be useful for us to take stock of our first six months of operation, and see what we can learn for the future. There can be no doubt, though, that our venture has been an amazing success. The business has taken off far faster than even our most optimistic forecasts and, with six retail outlets already up and running, we have made a really significant impact. Everyone, including all your respective teams, is very much to be congratulated.'

'And you too, Keith,' said Paul, 'your leadership and drive has been an inspiration.'

'Thank you, Paul,' responded Keith. 'We've all worked very hard. But how has it worked? Why have we been so successful?'

'I'm convinced that it's the attractiveness of our shops,' said Martin. 'I know that our merchandise is important, and our pricing must always be competitive but, if you ask me, I'd say that it's the design flair of the shops, coupled with the emphasis we put on looking after our customers. It doesn't matter how good our merchandise is, or how low our prices – if people aren't attracted into the shop in the first place, or if they feel uncomfortable as soon as they enter, we wouldn't sell a thing.'

'I think there's a lot of truth in that,' added Sam. 'Our shops are truly distinctive, and all our customer research shows that the attractiveness of the design, the ambience, the high quality of our staff all contribute to a much larger throughput of customers per day than our original estimates. The average spend is higher too.'

'Yes. That all makes good sense,' said Keith, nodding. 'And do you remember that discussion we had about six weeks after the first shop was opened? It was about whether or not to employ some more staff to cope with the additional unexpected volume of customers. Our accountants, I recall, advised that we should be cautious and not increase our overheads unduly, but the debate around this table was quite different – there was very strong support to maintain our policy of investing in people and customer service, and we all felt confident that the extra profits we had made in the first few weeks would fund the additional cost.'

'I remember that,' said Paul. 'That meeting got quite tense, and the accountants certainly gave us a hard time. But I'm sure our decision was right. The first branch went from strength to strength and provided the funds for the expansion programme.'

'Which took off like wildfire,' continued Sam. 'We opened the second branch after about ten weeks, then two more after about four months, and two more again just last week. It's fantastic!'

'It certainly is,' said Keith. 'I've been trying to represent what's been going on as a causal loop diagram. Does this make any sense?'

Keith went to the flipchart and copied the diagram from his scratch-pad.

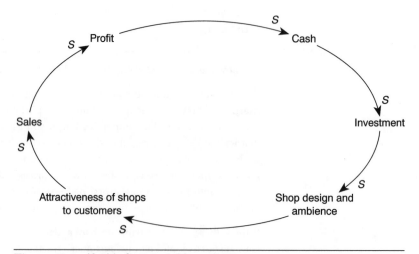

Figure 10.1 Keith's first causal loop diagram

'I know we've all done courses on this stuff, Keith,' said Paul, 'but I'd still appreciate your taking us through it.'

'OK,' replied Keith, 'let's start over here, with investment. As you all know, our original policy was to invest in shop design and ambience, including staff training and all that goes with it. The higher the level of investment, the higher the standards of design and so on, and that explains the *S* by the arrow head. The *S* stands for 'same', indicating that the two items on each end of the arrow move in the same direction: when investment goes up, so, in general, does the quality of the shop design.'

'And good shop design attracts customers. The better the design, the higher the traffic,' added Sam.

'Just so,' said Keith. 'Hence the *S* again.'

'And the rest is easy, isn't it?' said Paul. 'More customers generate more sales, giving more profit, and so generating more cash. This increases the funds available for investment, enabling us to improve our shops even more – just like the debate over whether or not to hire more staff. It's a perfect virtuous circle! That's just how our business has grown!'

'Yes,' said Sam. 'I agree. I really think, Keith, that you've captured what our business has done very perceptively.'

'Makes sense to me too,' added Martin. 'The only problem I see is how to manage the ever-increasing growth!'

'That would be a nice problem to have!' said Keith laughing.

Building consensus

This conversation between Keith and his colleagues is not yet over, and we shall return to it in the next chapter, but we'll interrupt our eavesdropping in order to highlight some features of the discussion so far.

Although the discussion has been artificially scripted, I trust you will feel that it is by no means unrealistic. Many business discussions take this form and they often remain at the level of debate and discussion. A special feature of this conversation, however, has been the manner in which Keith has captured the essence of the discussion in the form of a causal loop diagram.

At one level, this might be seen technically: the causal loop diagram might be regarded simply as a formal, structural representation of how the business has grown, suggesting that all we have to do now is apply a few numbers to enable us to build a forecasting model of how sales and profits will continue to grow in the future. This can indeed be done, for causal loop diagrams can form the basis for the construction of computer-based models which can do just that.

But the drawing of the causal loop diagram has done very much more than form the basis for a calculating engine, and to leave matters merely at the technical level misses something very important: the drawing of the causal loop diagram has had a behavioural impact too.

In drawing the diagram, Keith has established a mechanism for establishing consensus – or, alternatively, for demonstrating that there is no basis for consensus. The diagram serves as a focus of attention to which everyone in the team can relate and use to decide whether or not the diagram adequately captures their own views on how the business has grown. If they recognize it as something with which they agree they will say things like, 'Yes, that makes sense to me' or 'Yes, I see things that way, too'.

By contrast, anyone who considered that the growth of the business was not adequately represented by the diagram, would comment along the lines, 'I understand that, but I see things rather differently. Isn't the competitiveness of our pricing (or whatever) particularly important? And if it is, shouldn't that be captured somewhere on the diagram too?'. This would then lead to a discussion about pricing (or whatever), resulting perhaps in a rather different diagram.

To my mind, the building of consensus is a critical part of both management and building teams. What, for example, is the purpose of compiling a strategic plan? Is it to second-guess the future? Or to find the 'right' answer? Or is it to build a shared vision – a true consensus in which all the management team are firmly committed to an agreed set of goals?

Drawing a causal loop diagram is a very powerful way of asking the question 'Do you see the world in the same way as I do?' – a question which, I believe, lies at the heart of building consensus.

Mental models

Taking the discussion one step further, we might ask the question 'Just what is the consensus built on?'. To answer this question, let's look again at the conversation which led to the drawing of the causal loop diagram shown in Figure 10.1.

In compiling the causal loop diagram, Keith was capturing a chain of immediate cause-and-effect relationships, such as that between profit and sales. Provided the margin is reasonably independent of sales volume – a plausible enough assumption in many retail businesses – the causal relationship that profits increase as sales increase is pretty uncontentious, so there is no particular question of building consensus here.

But if we track back around the loop and ask the question 'What is the key driver of sales?', reference to the diagram shows the item 'attractiveness of shops to customers'. Whereas the link between 'profit' and 'sales' is almost a matter of accounting definition, the identification of 'attractiveness of shops to customers' as the key driver of 'sales' is, in essence, a matter of opinion or belief. True, the conversation refers to the evidence of customer research to support this, but even the most well conducted research can rarely give a definitive result: very often, opinions, beliefs and convictions play a very strong role in our determination of many cause-and-effect relationships – as we saw very explicitly in our earlier discussion of the drivers of motivation.

In general, of course, we could list – as you probably did when you tackled the 'Pause for thought' at the end of Chapter 9 – any number of drivers of sales, such as:

- competitive prices
- the intrinsic quality or uniqueness of the merchandise
- the effect of advertising or promotions
- the effect of endorsements, press coverage or public relations
- the energy of the shop staff in encouraging customers to buy
- the effect of the location of the shops
- the nature of the catchment area
- the absence of local competition

all of which are plausible, and which might act singly or in combination.

If we refer back to the conversation, we see that it was Martin who first suggested that the attractiveness of the stores was the key driver of sales, and he then went on to explain why he believed price and quality to be less important. The words he used were both natural and telling:

> 'I'm convinced that it's the attractiveness of our shops,' said Martin. 'I know that our merchandise is important, and our pricing must always be competitive but, if you ask me, I'd say that it's the design flair of the shops, coupled with the emphasis we put on looking after our customers. It doesn't matter how good our merchandise is, or how low our prices – if people aren't attracted into the shop in the first place, or if they feel uncomfortable as soon as they enter, we wouldn't sell a thing.'

These words are natural in the sense they ring reasonably true, realistical and telling in that he makes no attempt to hide the fact that he is speaking from conviction and belief – as implied by his phrases 'I'm convinced that . . .', and 'but if you ask me'.

In his bestselling book *The Fifth Discipline*, Peter Senge devotes many pages to the description and richer understanding of such beliefs which he calls *mental models* – a term which can also be found in Jay Forrester's original 1961 work *Industrial Dynamics*.

Mental models are very important, very powerful and very individual. They are expressions of how we view the world, of our assumptions, of our biases, of our beliefs. And every one of us is full of them. They are our own personal possessions and they influence our every action. They undoubtedly influenced your choices when you did the last 'Pause for thought', and many of my mental models are on conspicuous display throughout this book, especially as regards my views on the nature of teams. Usually, however, they are not discussed explicitly – when was the last time, for example, someone said to you 'Tell me about your mental models concerning immigration' or whatever? They are nonetheless profoundly important, for they influence our every action. And, although other people rarely say 'My mental model on this topic is . . .', you can often infer what their mental models are likely to be once you know what to look for. Whenever someone says 'I think . . .', 'I believe . . .', 'In my opinion . . .', 'Yes, I agree . . .' or whatever, a mental model is usually not far behind.

And, usually, people's mental models persist for considerable periods of time and imply consistent behaviours. Suppose, for example, that the Martin of our retail story had only recently joined Keith's company from another organization. Suppose further that Martin, in his previous company, had been discussing with another manager whether to allocate funds to shop refurbishment or to an advertising campaign. What do you think Martin's position would have been? Given that the mental model which he articulated stressed the importance he places on shop design and ambience, it is very likely that he would have been a strong advocate of shop refurbishment. But if the other manager had the firm belief – the mental model – that advertising was the key to success, they could have argued for a long time without reaching any agreement at all. And the argument would not really have been about the allocation of a budget: it would really have been about a difference in fundamental beliefs as to whether advertising or shop design were the dominant driver of sales. It would have been an argument about mental models.

The resolution of this postulated argument might have been to split the budget between the two camps, but this is not a true resolution – it is merely a pragmatic way of declaring a truce. After such an agreement, both individuals would still cherish their own personal beliefs. Research could possibly be carried out to try to determine which of the two views had greater validity, but this might be expensive, take considerable time, and might still be inconclusive. And even if it were to seem conclusive, would it have had any effect? Would the person whose mental model was 'disproved' change his mind, or would he challenge the evidence? Some people cling to their beliefs very tenaciously. Mental models run very deep.

Returning to our story, we now see that the cause-and-effect relationship between 'sales' and 'attractiveness of shops to customers' is the articulation of a mental model first proposed by Martin. What happened next?

> 'I think there's a lot of truth in that,' added Sam.

Here, Sam is agreeing that Martin's mental model aligns with her own. Sam had every opportunity to say 'I'm not too sure about that. To me . . .' or whatever, but she didn't: she immediately agreed with Martin. As, indeed, did Keith.

> 'Yes. That all makes good sense,' said Keith, nodding.

This too signifies that the mental model articulated originally by Martin is shared by Keith, but Keith went a step further when he added:

> 'And do you remember that discussion we had about six weeks after the first shop was opened? It was about whether or not to employ some more staff to cope with the additional volume. Our accountants, I recall, advised that we should be cautious, and not increase our overheads unduly, but the debate around this table was quite different – there was very strong support to maintain our policy of investing in people and customer service, and we all felt confident that the extra profits we had made in the first few weeks would fund the additional cost.'

In this part of the conversation. Keith is stating his belief that investment funds should be directed towards people and customer service – another mental model, and the one that underpins the link in the causal loop diagram between 'investment' and 'shop design and ambience'. Keith also takes the opportunity to remind the others that, at the time, they all agreed with this policy, which Paul then endorses as still valid.

> 'I remember that,' said Paul. 'That meeting got quite tense, and the accountants certainly gave us a hard time. But I'm sure our

decision was right. The first branch went from strength to strength and provided the funds for the expansion programme.'

To which Sam agreed.

Keith then summarized his understanding of the discussion with the causal loop diagram.

At one level, the causal loop diagram might appear to be a statement of the blindingly obvious, but this is not the case: there are many other feedback loops that might have been drawn working backwards from 'profit' and 'sales' – as you may well have discovered by comparing Figure 10.1 with your own response to the 'Pause for thought' at the end of Chapter 9. At a second level, the diagram might be regarded as no more than a quick representation of some key drivers of a retail business. But I believe (and here comes one of my mental models!) that the drawing of the diagram is working at two additional, much more profound, levels.

First, there is the level of the mental model itself. In drawing the diagram as he did, Keith captured three related mental models – one for each of the links between 'investment', 'shop design and ambience' and 'attractiveness of shops to customers'. And, given that mental models are personal, it is quite possible that the feedback loop you produced in response to the last 'Pause for thought' is quite different from Keith's. This is not a question of 'right' or 'wrong'; it is simply a question of 'different' – there is no law saying that you have to agree with Keith's view of the world. But, possibly, you do. In which case, you might, quite independently of Keith, have come up with a similar diagram. But maybe you didn't. Fine. Your mental models are different from Keith's.

This leads to the second, even deeper, level: the level of consensus. By drawing the diagram as a group activity, Keith is capturing not simply his own set of mental models, but the collective, shared mental models of the group. Given the nature of the discussion, and the general level of agreement, that was not too difficult, but had anyone not agreed they would have said so. The group's endorsement of the diagram signals that consensus has been reached, but now we can appreciate just what that consensus is. Consensus is a set of shared mental models.

PAUSE FOR THOUGHT

How would you define culture?

This 'Pause for thought' is hard: culture is one of the most difficult concepts to define. Most definitions, or maybe descriptions, express ideas such as 'the way we do things around here', or 'the organization's collective myths and legends'. I've never found these 'definitions' satisfactory – I've always found them too nebulous and too subjective. An alternative definition has been put forward by Peter Senge: 'the dominant set of shared mental models'. Although this definition is much harder to grasp, relying as it does not only on a familiarity with the concept of mental models but also on a deeper understanding of their significance, it is a definition which, to me, goes to the heart of the matter.

Each of us is driven by our mental models: they provide the context for our thoughts and guidelines for our actions, and our intuitive recognition of other people's mental models gives us a sense of comfort, or discomfort, in their company. Although mental models are rarely articulated explicitly, they can be perceived if you know what you are looking for, and they can be teased out, usually very safely, in an exercise to compile causal loop diagrams.

What Senge is suggesting is that groups of people who feel comfortable in each others' company will naturally share certain mental models. Indeed, if you consider your circle of friends, and the people you seek out at work, you might well agree that such groups naturally coalesce on this basis. Binding those groups together are unseen threads, sometimes reflecting a common, visible interest, such as cricket or making music, sometimes based on the very soft notion that you enjoy being in that group. But where does that enjoyment – that comfort – come from? Peter Senge suggests that it derives from an intuitive, often unstated, natural and unforced sharing of your mental models with theirs.

In larger groups, such as organizations, although there is likely to be a wide diversity of mental models, certain mental models, for whatever reason, become dominant – for example, mental models about dress, about the protocols for who can telephone whom, about the order in which names are written on circulation lists for documents, about working practices, about the relationship between 'professionals' and 'support staff', and about criteria for success and promotion. Much of this is unwritten, and people new to the organization soon detect what is going on. If their own mental models naturally 'fit', that's fine, but if they don't, they have a choice to conform – either by changing their personal mental models, or by suppressing them (in which case tension very often arises) – or to leave.

This process is itself a feedback loop: those who fit, stay; those who don't, go. And so a set of mental models becomes dominant, and can persist for a long time, particularly as managers recruit and promote their juniors in their own image.

There is clearly a chicken-and-egg issue here – where does the original set of dominant mental models come from? It often derives from the original leadership, in which a strong, determined and charismatic leader stamps his or her mark on an organization by indoctrinating, not necessarily unwillingly, their cohorts. The presence of the dominant mental models can then exert considerable pressure on others, and the process becomes self-perpetuating.

To me, Senge's insight is powerful. It relates well to my own experience, and the concept of a dominant set of shared mental models is far more tangible than the nebulous 'the way we do things around here'.

If, as Erich Segal said in his novel *Love Story* that 'Love is never having to say you're sorry', then surely 'Consensus is the collective and willing acceptance of a group mental model' – the recognition that your mental models are in harmony with other people's. And, to me, that is the most fundamental underpinning of teamwork that you could wish to have.

And so, back to teamwork

We have, at last, come full circle, and, given that the central concept we are discussing is the feedback loop, what could be more appropriate?

We started this part of our journey in Chapter 8, with the anecdote from Michael Caine's film *The Italian Job*, in which he said that teamwork meant doing things his way. We then travelled from 1960s' Italy back to Ancient Greece where Plato and Socrates were musing about elephants and wine, and from there to 1950s' Cambridge, Massachusetts where Jay Forrester and his colleagues were busy developing systems thinking – a method of describing complex systems in terms of feedback loops. We then saw that, in the process of teasing out the structure of feedback loops, people naturally express their underlying beliefs, opinions and judgements – their mental models.

It has been a long and involved journey, so let's take this moment to draw breath, reflect, and summarize.

TEAMWORK

Let's deal first with the issue of teamwork. Why, in a book on innovation, are we looking at teamwork? For these reasons:

- Although innovation can come from oneself, it is much more likely to spring from group interactions.
- Not only do groups bring a richer variety of experiences, but the process of group interaction, when taking place positively and supportively, is much more conducive to the processes of challenge, provocation and the creation of new patterns than anything we can do by ourselves.
- In normal everyday speech, we use the word 'team' to denote a group which reaches an enhanced level of performance. This is why we speak of 'football teams' rather than 'football groups'.
- 'Teams' will therefore be intrinsically better at innovation than mere 'groups'.
- So it makes sense to gain a better understanding of teamwork.

OF ELEPHANTS . . .

What of the elephant anecdote? The take-home messages here are:

- Certain types of 'system', as represented by the elephant, are a complex whole, formed from the intimate relationship between very many highly interconnected component parts.
- If we wish to understand how such a system works, our normal approach – to break the system down into its component parts and study those in detail – is doomed to failure: cutting the system up immediately destroys the intrinsic connectedness, the essence of the system of interest. Conventional analytical approaches won't work: to understand complex interconnected systems, we need a different approach.
- And since systems containing human beings – such as societies, organizations and teams – are highly interconnected, such a different approach, if we can discover it, might throw light on teamwork and many other things too.

. . . AND WINE

And so to the wine anecdote:

- At first sight, many situations appear to be linear, with a beginning and an end, and operating in the context of apparently very straightforward cause-and-effect relationships.

- Such a view is often very simplistic.
- A more fundamental description may often be expressed in terms of one or more feedback loops, in which all the component parts are interconnected within a unified whole.
- Within a feedback loop, the concept of causality is subtle. A statement such as 'A causes B' might indeed be a statement of truth, but not the whole truth: because of the interconnected nature of the feedback loop, sooner or later and somehow or other, there will be some way in which B in turn influences A, and in which B can be regarded as a cause of A.
- Feedback loops are everywhere but, perhaps because they are so much part of our everyday life, we rarely notice them.

SYSTEMS THINKING

The recognition of the existence, and importance, of feedback loops then led to the introduction to 'systems thinking':

- Systems thinking is a method of describing complex systems, usually in terms of feedback loops.
- Systems thinking does not attempt to dissect complex problems in order to study the component parts; rather, systems thinking embraces and accepts complexity and connectedness and suggests that we will gain insight into this complexity and connectedness by discovering the underlying feedback loops and examining their collective behaviours.
- Systems thinking therefore represents an alternative to conventional analysis – an alternative which is well suited to the study of complex, interconnected systems that involve people and teams.

CAUSAL LOOP DIAGRAMS

We then saw that one of the key tools in systems thinking is the causal loop diagram:

- A causal loop diagram represents the key elements of a problem in terms of one or more interconnected feedback loops.
- The elements of a causal loop diagram are not constrained to real, tangible physical or measurable objects such as 'temperature', 'sales volume' or 'profit', but may include whatever concepts are relevant to the problem of interest, however intangible, conceptual or unmeasurable.

We next examined the process by which causal loop diagrams can be compiled:

- To construct a causal loop diagram to explore how to achieve an objective, it is often helpful to work 'backwards' around the diagram, teasing out the immediate causality driving each particular item by asking 'What drives . . .?' or 'What causes . . .?'. If the issue is one exploring the consequences of policy, it is usually easier to work forwards by asking 'What are the consequences of . . .?'.
- Sometimes, the answer to the question 'What drives . . .?' or 'What causes . . .?' or 'What are the consequences of . . .?' is a matter of definition, fact or data; very often however, it is more a matter of judgement, opinion or belief.
- In articulating these judgements, opinions and beliefs, we are also articulating our 'mental models'.

MENTAL MODELS

And so to mental models:

- Mental models are important and very personal.
- They influence many of our daily decisions and actions.
- They are rarely explicitly stated, and are often very private.
- The process of creating a causal loop diagram is usually a safe way of allowing our mental models to be expressed.
- Individuals can capture their own mental models on their own causal loop diagrams, and the study of other people's causal loop diagrams can show you the extent to which other people think like you do and the extent to which your mental models are instinctively shared – or not.
- Alternatively, groups can collaborate on creating a collective causal loop diagram, expressing their shared mental models. This process works well when the mental models are spontaneously in harmony, but less well when they are in conflict.
- A group reaches consensus when each individual member of the group is willing to accept the collective, shared mental model.
- A group is a team when the process of reaching consensus is natural, spontaneous and unforced on a wide variety of issues, thereby empowering the team to reach a superior level of performance.

AND BACK TO TEAMS

The conclusion we reach is that teamwork is very much about the depth and breadth of the mental models naturally and spontaneously shared by a number of different people. This does not imply that successful teams must necessarily be identical clones; rather that the individuals in a high-performing team have a natural, spontaneous and unforced mutual overlap in their mental models which enables them to achieve success both individually and collectively.

Sometimes, the discovery of the natural overlap of mental models happens by chance, and this is one of the underlying drivers of friendship. In the workplace, however, people are often thrown together almost arbitrarily and then expected to behave as 'teams'. Sometimes this works reasonably easily; but sometimes, as we all know, it doesn't. However, with the insights gained from systems thinking, there may be ways of helping the teambuilding process by allowing prospective team members to gain a deeper understanding of both their own mental models and those of their colleagues, so that the extent of natural overlap can be better understood. This suggests that it may well be worthwhile having a deeper grasp of systems thinking, as we shall achieve in the following two chapters.

But if teamwork is about the natural overlap of mental models, does that imply that I can only be a successful member of a team in which my mental models are naturally accepted? My immediate answer to this question is 'Yes'. But underpinning this question is the assumption that my mental models are fixed, unchanging and unchangeable. What if my mental models are adaptable or can be changed? If they can be, then perhaps I could naturally fit in to a wider diversity of teams. Similarly, perhaps other people's mental models can change too, enabling wider, more diverse groups to work more harmoniously together. What, then, might be done to influence mental models – both mine and other people's? How would you describe the process of changing or modifying a mental model? I'm not sure, but maybe *learning* has something to do with it – not learning in terms of remembering multiplication tables, but learning at the much deeper level of appreciating someone else's world-view, adapting my behaviours to new circumstances, taking on new ideas – innovation even!

PAUSE FOR THOUGHT

What do you think is the real acid test for teamwork?

How about resolving conflict?

And why, when faced with conflict, do high-performing teams avoid bickering and back-biting, but resolve conflict quickly and professionally?

11 STRUCTURES

Virtuous circles

We'll return to the issues of teamwork, mental models and learning in the next chapter; the purpose of this chapter is to develop our understanding of systems thinking further, so that we can feel confident we can construct causal loop diagrams, and gain an intuitive understanding of how the systems captured in such diagrams are likely to behave.

A useful starting point is the causal loop diagram drawn by Keith to describe their retail business, as shown in Figure 10.1 and reproduced again here as Figure 11.1.

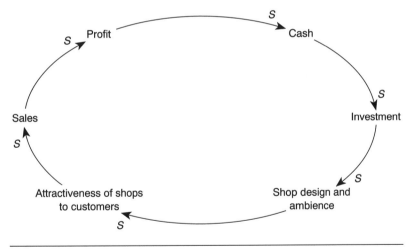

Figure 11.1　Keith's first causal loop diagram

This diagram represents what Keith and his colleagues believe to be the underlying drivers of their business and, as we saw in Chapter 10, captures the management team's collective mental model. No business is static, however, and we would expect key items such as sales, profit and cash to change over time: indeed, much of the management task is to adopt policies, take actions and make decisions so that items such as the cash balance evolve in a specific, targeted and controlled way. Given the structure as represented in Figure 11.1, how do you think the cash balance will evolve over time? Try the next 'Pause for thought'.

PAUSE FOR THOUGHT

Suppose that the business represented by Figure 11.1 currently has a cash balance of £50 000. Suppose, too, that you agree that Figure 11.1 is a good representation of the business.

How do you think the cash balance will evolve over, say, the next four years?

Don't try to make numerical estimates: try to visualize the shape of a graph.

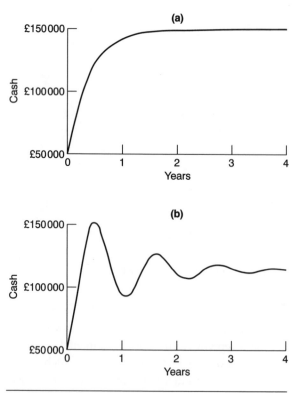

Figure 11.2 How does the cash balance evolve over time?

When I ask this question in my workshops and seminars, the responses usually describe one of the following four shapes:

- a profile which rises, and then flattens out, as depicted by the graph shown in Figure 11.2(a)
- a graph that rises and then wobbles, perhaps flattening out, as in Figure 11.2(b), or perhaps not
- a linear graph, as in Figure 11.2(c) or
- an upwards curving shape, as in Figure 11.2(d).

Occasionally, a different shape appears, but most people usually draw one of these four shapes or a close variant.

Let's go back to the causal loop diagram, and think it through. The argument goes like this.

If the cash balance rises, this increases the funds for investment, which in turn increases the opportunity to improve the ambience of the shops,

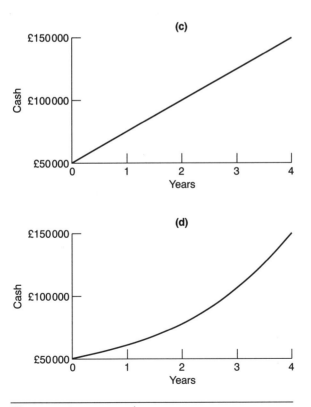

Figure 11.2 *continued*

which stimulates increased customer traffic, driving up sales, increasing profits and adding further to the cash balance. With each turn of the circle the cash balance therefore becomes increasingly larger and larger. This is a story of unlimited growth.

This rules out graphs such as Figure 11.2(a), which show initial growth followed by a steady state. The issue here is not the initial growth, but whether or not the system can evolve to an eventual steady state. If you refer to the causal loop diagram of Figure 11.1, and the corresponding interpretation of the preceding paragraph, you will see that the causal loop implies that growth goes on and on, without limit, for ever. So there is nothing in the causal loop diagram that will lead to a tailing off: growth never stops.

'That's crazy,' you might say. 'Nothing can grow for ever and ever.' That may indeed be true but, in this context, that is not quite the point: the point is the interpretation of the causal loop diagram shown in Figure 11.1 which, as we have seen, implies unlimited growth. The (valid) point that nothing can grow for ever cannot be inferred from the causal loop diagram as depicted in Figure 11.1; rather, it is an insight which suggests that the causal loop diagram of Figure 11.1 is not a complete description of reality – a point to which we shall return in the next chapter. For the moment, though, we are not addressing that issue but, rather, 'How does the causal loop of Figure 11.1 behave?'. The answer to this question is 'as a depiction of unlimited growth'. This rules out a behaviour such as that shown in Figure 11.2(a) and, by the same token, that in Figure 11.2(b).

That leaves Figures 11.2(c) and 11.2(d), both of which show unlimited growth. How do we choose between the two? Figure 11.2(c) shows linear growth, in which the cash balance increases in a straight line; Figure 11.2(d) shows non-linear growth, in which the cash balance becomes increasingly larger, causing the graph to curve upwards.

Let's assume that the cash balance starts at a value of £50 000. If, over the first year, the net cash inflow is, say, a further £10 000, then the cash balance at the end of the year, and hence at the start of the next year, will be £60 000. If growth is linear, £10 000 of cash continues to flow in every year, implying that the cash balance at the start of the following year will be £70 000, rising to £80 000 the year after that, and so on.

Can this be the case? If we refer to the causal loop diagram, we see that the year-on-year increase in cash is driven by that year's profit: indeed, for many retail businesses, the net cash flow is often very nearly equal to the accounting profit, excluding depreciation. And, following the causal loop diagram back, we see that this year's profit is linked ultimately to the year-start cash balance. This in turn implies that the year-on-year increase in cash is determined by the cash balance at the start of the year, and so the bigger the cash balance, the bigger the increase in cash over the year. This is, of course, exactly what you would expect, for this is what feedback loops are all about. But if the year-on-year increase in cash is determined by the opening cash balance which is itself increasing, then the year-on-year cash increase cannot be constant, but must get bigger and bigger. Growth is therefore not linear, and the graph shown in Figure 11.2(c) cannot be the correct description of how the cash balance will evolve over time. Rather, the year-on-year increase in cash gets steadily bigger, pushing the cash balance up ever more strongly, curving the graph upwards as shown in Figure 11.2(d).

Exponential growth

We now see that the time behaviour of the feedback loop shown in Figure 11.1 may be represented by a graph showing ever-increasing growth, just like the upward-sloping curve of Figure 11.2(d). In principle, the growth continues for ever, since the feedback loop includes nothing to stop the unceasing spinning of the virtuous circle; the growth is not linear, but curved, by virtue of the causality implied by the feedback loop – this year's cash balance influences next year's which in turn influences the year after and so on.

This form of non-linear growth is familiar as that associated with compound interest, but it arises in many other circumstances too, the most obvious example being population growth – the size of the population today determines the size next year. It is known by mathematicians as *exponential* growth and is very common, largely because it is the natural consequence of feedback loops like the one shown in Figure 11.1. Many natural processes may be represented by such a feedback loop and, even though different processes will have different starting points and different growth rates, all will show exponential growth.

This is a very powerful statement, and it represents one of the most important insights of systems thinking. What it says is that *the structure of the feedback loop determines its generic behaviour*: all feedback loops with the structure of Figure 11.1 behave in the same generic way – they all exhibit exponential growth. Some will grow faster than others – for the specific numbers associated with any system will vary from system to system – but none of them will grow linearly, nor to a limit, nor will they oscillate. They grow and grow and grow.

PAUSE FOR THOUGHT

Imagine you are a frog, living on the edge of a pond with many other frogs. Way on the other side of the pond is a lily pad. For many years, the community of frogs and the lily pad live harmoniously with each other. But, one day, some industrial effluent flows into the pond and causes the lily pad to start growing much, much faster – as a result of the pollution, the lily pad doubles in size every day.

Now this poses quite a threat to the frogs. If ever the lily pad should cover the entire pond, the frogs will no longer be able to feed properly, and will surely die.

- **How would you describe the mode of growth of the lily pad?**
- **If the entire pond is covered 50 days after the pollution incident, how many days are there between the pond being half-covered and disaster?**
- **Suppose the frogs require five days to identify the threat, think about it, discuss it, decide to take action and then act. How much (approximately) of the pond's surface is covered on the last day before they are inevitably doomed?**

This 'Pause for thought' highlights one of the very alarming features of exponential growth. When exponential growth gets going, it really gets going. The growth of the lily pad is, of course, exponential: the information that the pads double in size every 24 hours implies a feedback loop in which tomorrow's population of lily pads is twice today's – this being the now familiar sign of exponential growth.

If you answered '25' to the question 'How many days are there between the pond being half-covered and disaster', then you are not alone. Most people do. But the correct answer is day one. If the lily pad doubles itself every 24 hours, then you have only one day between half-covered and totally covered. Most people tend to think that half-covered equates to half the time, but that is linear growth not exponential growth. Exponential growth catches up with you fast – really fast. So fast, you often don't notice it. As the next question demonstrates.

If the frogs require 5 days to decide to take action, and then to act, then the latest day on which this process can begin is day 45: if they start any later than this, the lily pads will surely overwhelm them before their action has taken effect. The frogs are therefore doomed after day 45 – there is absolutely nothing that can be done thereafter. Now, most people think that, at day 45, the fraction of the pond covered by lily pads is 45/50, or 90 per cent.

But the answer isn't 90 per cent. That figure implies linear growth, not exponential growth. So, what is the answer?

The easiest way to determine the correct answer is to work backwards. With one day to go, as we have seen, the pond is one-half covered; with two days, it is one half of one half, or one quarter; with three days, it is one half of one quarter, or one eighth; with four days to go, one half of one eighth, or one sixteenth; and, with the critical five days to go, the pond is just one half of one sixteenth covered – one thirty-second, or just a little more than 3 per cent.

Can you imagine the debate at the frog council on that morning? Cassandra Frog gets up and makes an impassioned plea that immediate action must be taken: the young tadpoles must be evacuated forthwith, the adult frogs must start eating lily pads like there is no tomorrow for, as of five days' time, there will be no tomorrow – the pond will be covered and they will all surely die.

Can you imagine how poor Cassandra Frog is shouted down as a worrier, a pessimist, an alarmist?

Have you ever experienced a meeting like that?

But if the frogs take no action, they will surely die, for in the next five days, the lily pads will grow and grow. Exponentially. And that means fast. Really fast.

Now, because exponential – not linear – growth is the natural behaviour of many feedback loops, and feedback loops of this type are everywhere, this type of situation is very common. But, for the most part, we are ill-equipped to handle it. There are two reasons for this.

First, although exponential growth is exceptionally fast, it doesn't start out like that. In fact, it starts really, really slowly. As an example, think about how much of the pond is covered by the lily pads on, say, days 8, 9 and 10 of the story. The percentage of the area covered on each of these days is, respectively, given by $100/2^{42}$, $100/2^{41}$ and $100/2^{40}$. These numbers are really infinitesimally small – far too tiny for your calculator to recognize. It is only when we are well into the last ten days of the 50 that the lily pads are at all noticeable. Before that, the frogs live in blissful ignorance.

So, pause for a moment and reflect upon issues such as population growth, pollution, deforestation, global warming, the ozone layer, AIDS and even the infestation of Lake Victoria in East Africa by the water hyacinth plant – a true-life example of the lily pad story, but with the local population as the frogs. There are an enormous number of natural phenomena whose behaviours can be perceptively described in terms of feedback loops just like that drawn by Keith to describe the growth of his retail business. For the great power of systems thinking is that the dynamic behaviour of the system depends on the structure of the feedback loop, rather than on its details. Just as Keith's retail business grows exponentially, so does deforestation. And it all starts very, very slowly – so slowly, you hardly notice.

Ever felt like a frog?

But that's not the only problem. You see, it's not just a question of growth . . .

But virtuous circles can be vicious too

What goes up, as they say, must come down, and there is no law saying that profits must increase. They might decrease, and the business might make a loss. If a loss does happen, the cash balance will drop

PAUSE FOR THOUGHT

Turn back to Figure 11.1, and take another look at this now very familiar feedback loop.

Suppose that, for whatever reason, in a particular year, the business makes a loss. What happens?

correspondingly. But, according to the causal loop diagram, cash is linked to investment, and the *S* on the arrow linking 'cash' to 'investment' means that these two items move in the same direction. So, if the cash balance goes down, investment is cut back, our premises may not receive the new carpet we had intended, our once appealing shops are no longer quite as attractive to customers as they once were, sales slacken off, further losses are made, even more cash is lost from the business, and so we have to cut back even harder on investment . . .

Suddenly, our virtuous circle has turned nasty. Vicious, even.

But it's the same structure. Nothing has changed in the feedback loop – all the items are still the same, the arrows of causality still point in the same directions and the *S* indicators are still all *S*s. The only difference is the way we kicked the circle off.

Being optimists, our first thoughts are all about growth: what happens when profits increase? And, sure enough, the virtuous circle spins away, growing exponentially for ever. But if we start the loop with a loss, the circle continues to spin, but this time each turn reinforces decline rather than growth. The circle is a vicious one, which spins exponentially fast – so fast that, once we are in decline, we may not be able to stop it. We're as helpless as the frogs.

The vicious circle spirals away for ever. This can be represented graphically, implying that the question 'How does the causal loop shown in

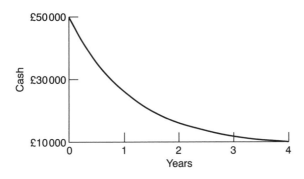

Figure 11.3 But the cash balance can decline too

Figure 11.1 behave?' has not one, but two, answers – exponential growth, as we have already seen, but also exponential decline, as shown in Figure 11.3.

The take-home message here is that the *same* feedback loop structure can support both growth and decline – it's simply a matter of how the loop is set spinning or how the loop can be set spinning the other way if it is subject to some external shock.

Suppose, for example, that a business starts off growing well, with the feedback loop spinning away merrily in growth mode. But then something unexpected occurs which trips the loop the other way, causing sudden unexpected and catastrophic decline. Bust follows boom. The growth business suddenly fails. The rising star suddenly falls . . .

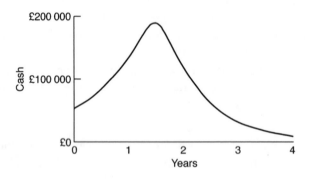

Figure 11.4 Boom and bust

The history of business is littered with such stories. That of People's Express, an airline that reaped the early benefits of the deregulation of the air transportation industry in the United States has been very well documented, and forms the basis of one of the Harvard Business School's case studies. Very briefly, their growth was so rapid, and demand became so overwhelming, that their service quality became so severely eroded that customers left them as quickly as they had originally flocked in. So quickly, in fact, that the airline did not have time to react before the decline became fatal. Another example is that of Ratner's jewellers. Gerald Ratner was an icon of Britain in the Thatcherite 1980s – a self-made man who built an empire of jewellery shops. One evening, whilst being fêted at a business dinner, he gave a speech in which he made a flippant and derogatory remark about his products which was widely reported in the press. The remark offended core customers who then decided not to visit his shops any more. Bust followed boom very quickly here too.

Reinforcing loops

We've spent a lot of time studying the feedback loop of Figure 11.1, and for good reason – feedback loops of this type are extremely common. We now know that the loop behaves as a virtuous or a vicious circle, depending on which way it is triggered, and the resulting growth or decline is not linear but exponential. As the story of the frogs demonstrated, it is difficult to gain an intuitive feel for exponential growth – at one moment nothing seems to be happening, and then we are overwhelmed.

Why is it, then, that the loop of Figure 11.1 behaves in this way? Is it some attribute of the problem of retailing? Was it caused by one of our mental models – for example, the belief that the attractiveness of the shops is a key driver of sales?

The answer to both of these questions is 'no'. The exponential growth, or decline, implied by the feedback loop is not a result of the specifics of the retail problem nor the details of any of the underlying mental models: the behaviour of the loop is driven by the *structure* of the loop itself. And by structure, I mean the relationships between the items as determined by the pattern of *S*s (for items that move in the same direction) or *O*s (for items that move in opposite directions).

Consider, as a further example, the feedback loop shown in Figure 11.5. Following this loop around, an increase in A drives an increase in B, which in turn increases C, cascading on to D, which feeds back to increase A again. It does not matter what A, B, C, D (and, for that matter, E, F and G) are: any loop with this structure shows exponential growth or decline.

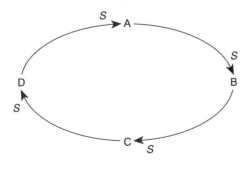

Figure 11.5 A reinforcing loop

Given that there are many natural examples of feedback loops with the structure of Figure

11.5, from business growth to populations, it is useful to refer to it as an *archetype* – a structure that occurs often, either on its own or in combination with other features. This archetype is commonly referred to as a *reinforcing loop* in which, as the name signifies, the behaviour is reinforced on each turn, thereby encompassing both growth and decline.

Figure 11.6 is a variant on Figure 11.5, in which the links from B to C, and from D back to A, are shown as *O*s rather than *S*s and provokes another 'Pause for thought'.

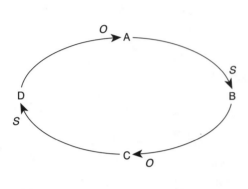

Figure 11.6   How does this loop behave?

PAUSE FOR THOUGHT

How does the loop shown in Figure 11.6 behave?

Following the loop around from A, as A increases B increases, but this time an increase in B causes a *de*crease in C. But as C decreases, D also decreases (the *S* implies that D moves in the same direction as C, be it up or down) and, as D decreases, A now *in*creases, for the *O* linking D back to A indicates that D and A move in opposite directions. The overall result is that an initial increase in A generates a further increase in A, and so the loop shows exponential growth or decline.

Figure 11.6 is therefore also a valid representation of a reinforcing loop, just like Figure 11.5. It also gives us an easy way of identifying whether or not any loop behaves as a reinforcing loop: just count the number of *O*s. If there are an even number of *O*s (zero is an even number), then the loop must be a reinforcing loop. Always. Any pair of *O*s in the same loop will cancel each other out, even if they are not adjacent. Once again, we return to the fundamental truth that the dynamic behaviour of a feedback loop is determined by its structure not its content.

Balancing loops

As a further example, study the generic loop represented by Figure 11.7.

How does this one behave?

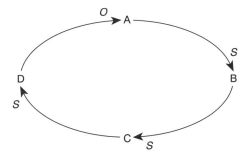

Figure 11.7 And this one?

The loop in Figure 11.7 has only one *O*, so it can't be a reinforcing loop. A feel for the behaviour can be gained by following the loop around in the normal way: an increase in A causes an increase in B, which in turn increases C and then D. An *in*crease in D, however, causes a *de*crease in A, implying that the original increase in A is counteracted by the effect of D once the loop has had time to come into effect. Similarly, if A were originally to decrease, the effect of D on A would be to bring about an increase.

In the case of a reinforcing loop, an original increase on A causes a further increase with each turn of the wheel, so bringing about exponential growth or decline in a process known as *positive feedback*. The loop of Figure 11.7, however, behaves rather differently: the influence of D on A is to dampen the original change in A: no matter whether A increased or decreased, the effect of D is to counteract the original change, as if the loop is trying to cause A to return to its original value. This is an example of *negative feedback*, and the archetype illustrated by Figure 11.7 is known as a *balancing loop* or *control loop* in recognition of the way it tries to maintain a balance by resisting changes to the value of A, or controlling A to remain at a particular value. Whereas reinforcing loops have an even number of *O*s, balancing loops have an odd number.

Balancing loops are also very common, and we have already encountered two examples: one was the shower, in which the feedback loop acts to control the water to the desired temperature; the other was the original example of Socrates pouring the wine into the glass, illustrated in Figure 11.8.

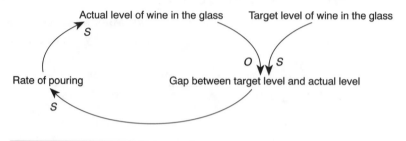

Figure 11.8   An example of a balancing loop

As can be seen, the loop in Figure 11.8 contains just one *O*, so it must be a balancing loop. Often, balancing loops are associated with the achievement of a goal or a target, and this is represented by the item 'Target level of wine in the glass'. This captures Socrates' objective of whether he wants the wine glass full to the brim, half-full or whatever.

At any instant, the wine in the glass is at a given 'actual' level, and the transfer of information from the wine glass to his brain enables Socrates to make a continuous assessment of whether or not he has reached his goal. Mentally, he is always measuring the gap between the current actual state and the desired target state. For a given actual level, the higher the target, the greater the gap, hence the *S* linking the target to the gap; for a given target, the higher the actual level, the lower the gap, hence the *O*. Having mentally established the gap, Socrates then adjusts his rate of pouring, and the *S* here captures the likelihood that the greater the gap, the greater his rate of pouring and, conversely, the smaller the gap between the target and the actual level, the slower the rate of pouring. Finally, the greater the rate of pouring, the greater the actual level of wine in the glass, hence the *S* here, and the loop is closed.

That explanation is somewhat wordy and perhaps rather unreal: we don't usually think of the 'target level of wine in the glass' or the 'gap between target and actual'. But the fact that we don't think of them doesn't imply that they're not there: Figure 11.8 represents an informed description of what is going on, however unconscious the actions may be.

Some balancing loops, however, are very much part of our consciousness. In business, for example, exactly the same feedback loop applies: budgets represent goals and targets, and you probably don't need me to tell you how much time you and your colleagues spend examining variances, and trying to ensure that your actual performance reaches your goal.

Dangles

Look at the item labelled 'Target level of wine in the glass' in Figure 11.8. As can be seen, it connects into the loop but is otherwise dangling – there are no arrows driving it. This seems to break one of the fundamental rules of systems thinking: that everything must be connected, somehow, to everything else.

Well, not quite everything. There is a class of items, of which this is a representative example, which can be allowed to dangle. Let me explain why.

The issue is primarily one of boundaries – what is inside the system of interest and what is outside. This, by the way, is not a negation of the very important principle of taking a complete, holistic view; rather, it is a recognition that even the most complex system has boundaries somewhere. Yes, it is important to ensure that we do not dissect the system itself, but that is not in conflict with the existence of natural boundaries. Take the elephant, for example. If we wish to understand the workings of the elephant, we must not cut it in half. But the whole elephant has a natural boundary, so why not use it to distinguish between the system of interest (the elephant), and other things that might be of general interest but not just now (the rest of the world). If, however, the system of interest were the elephant in the context of its environment, then defining the boundary of the system as the skin of the elephant would not be appropriate – in this case we need to include the jungle too. So, system boundaries depend on context.

How does this relate to the dangling item 'target level of wine in the glass'? If we follow the normal systems thinking procedure, to trace this back we ask a question such as 'What are the drivers of the target level of the glass?', to which the response is something like 'It's what Socrates wants', which in turn is driven by, say, 'level of thirst', and so on back. This shows that it *is* possible to trace a chain of causality back from 'target level of wine in the glass' and that, sooner or later, we will define another feedback loop. This train of thought follows Socrates' motivation and might indeed be relevant in some, but not necessarily all, contexts. If our system of interest is primarily the act of controlling the level of wine in the glass, the target level of wine is very important but the driving motivation need not be. So we define the boundary there.

The existence of a single dangling item is, in fact, a very common feature of balancing loops. Implicit in every balancing loop is a goal, an objective, a target or an externally imposed limit. In this case, it is the desired level of wine in the glass; in another case, it might be the preferred temperature of a shower; in a business context, it might be a target level of sales, costs or profit as expressed in a budget. The loop then acts – with our intervention – to drive the actual level of the wine, temperature of the shower or performance of the business towards the desired goal.

In the context of the system described by the balancing loop, the goal is an externality – something imposed on the loop from outside, which the action of the loop has to strive to achieve. Most middle managers, who struggle daily to achieve their budgets, will empathize with that concept.

So, dangles are allowed, but, in general:

- they must relate to externally imposed limits, goals, targets, objectives or desires
- they should relate only to balancing loops
- they should be few in number, not more than one for each balancing loop.

Lags

A further feature of the balancing loop shown in Figure 11.8 is less obvious, for it concerns time. We have already talked about time in the context of reinforcing loops, where we saw that the time behaviour of such loops may be described in terms of exponential growth or decline, as expressed in terms of the graphs shown in Figures 11.2(d) and 11.3.

The time behaviour of a balancing loop typically shows one of two rather different patterns. In the case of Socrates and the wine, the level of the wine steadily rose to meet the target, as represented by the graph shown in Figure 11.9.

If, however, we recall the example of controlling the water in an unfamiliar shower, the time behaviour is rather different as illustrated by Figure 11.10. In this case, the temperature ends up at the required level, but it does not approach that level smoothly: rather it overshoots, then undershoots, oscillates for a while and then homes in.

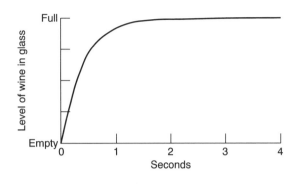

Figure 11.9 A balancing loop in action

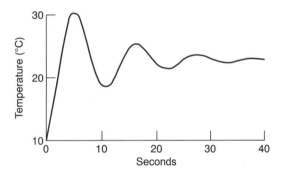

Figure 11.10 Time lags can often lead to oscillatory behaviour, as in this example of setting the temperature of a shower

Both the smooth (Figure 11.9) and oscillatory (Figure 11.10) behaviours are characteristic of balancing loops, and the distinction between them usually depends on how long it takes for the feedback loop to spin. Some feedback loops operate very quickly, an example being our natural action of pouring; others have quite considerable time delays and these tend to lead to oscillations. As the example of the unfamiliar shower demonstrates, the oscillations can easily be aggravated by our own behaviour: if we do not recognize the inherent time delays in the system, or if we are too impatient, we tend to intervene and overcorrect, causing the oscillations to swing more wildly and last for longer before they settle down. That's why the temperature in the shower becomes so erratic and why inexperienced drivers oversteer in skids. And the same phenomenon happens in business when people overreact because budgets aren't being met. Let alone what happens in the economy when the government is trying to enact policies to meet targets on inflation, unemployment or exchange rates.

When trying to manage a system composed of variables interconnected in very complex ways by feedback loops, it is oh-so-tempting to take 'decisive action' to 'correct' the observed behaviour in order to achieve a given target. If the loops themselves and the time lags are poorly understood, any interventions are at best blind and at worst totally, and often inadvertently, counterproductive. One of the most important insights into the behaviour of an oscillating balancing loop is to leave well alone until it reaches the goal of its own accord – as it will certainly do if you have the patience. Blind intervention will often make the oscillations more violent, and changing the target (say, by revising the budget) often causes another set of oscillations, but about a new goal.

Engineers in general, and electrical engineers in particular, will be familiar with this discussion of negative feedback balancing loops. Control theory and control engineering are based on these concepts, and many of the devices which we use in everyday life (such as thermostats), as well as those which we thankfully do not use in everyday life (such as guided missiles) depend on them. Yes, systems thinking is no more than an enhancement of control theory, in which the scope of application is much broader.

This, of course, is no accident. Jay Forrester, the originator of systems thinking, was trained as an electrical engineer, and so was well versed in applying control theory to technical problems. What he spotted was that the same mode of thinking could be successfully transferred to a much wider range of problems, so he applied the same basic techniques – such as feedback loops – to a series of different contexts.

Yes, we are back to patterns: this is exactly the same as the difference between Beethoven and the Beatles and between Shakespeare and Steinbeck as discussed in Chapter 2. Forrester took control theory from the discipline of engineering, disaggregated it back to its component parts of causality and feedback, and applied the results to problems of business, sociology and politics. Another example of innovation in action!

Some important insights

As we have seen, reinforcing loops have an even number of Os, and balancing loops contain an odd number of Os. This leads to yet another profound insight. Any loop must have either an even or odd number of Os – there are no other possibilities. So any single loop must be either a reinforcing loop or a balancing loop.

The fact that every single feedback loop in the world must behave in one of just two ways is quite startling, and makes a significant contribution to our goal of understanding complexity. This is indeed a profound insight. But remember that there is no law saying that all problems can be adequately described by a single feedback loop: as we shall see, most real world problems are characterized by multiple loops, all interacting with each other in many different ways.

A further important insight emerges from another fact that we have already examined – namely, that the dynamic behaviour of a feedback loop is determined by its structure, as opposed to its specific content. Generically, all reinforcing loops have the structure of Figure 11.5 and behave in the same way, growing or declining without limit. The specifics of how fast growth or decline occurs will differ from case to case, but the underlying behaviour will be the same: inexorable growth or decline. Likewise, all balancing loops have the structure of Figure 11.7 and tend towards the specified target or goal, either smoothly, as depicted in Figure 11.9, or after some oscillations, as depicted in Figure 11.10.

The insight is this: *if you want to change the behaviour of a system, you have to change its structure.* Simply tinkering around with specific items will have no significant effect: you can wiggle the regulator of the hotel's shower until the cows come home but the water temperature will continue to oscillate. From a managerial standpoint, this is a truly vital point for, given a complex system comprising many interacting feedback loops called 'our business', how can we, as managers, intervene wisely to achieve the goals we seek, avoid unstable effects such as wild oscillations and avoid quick fixes that backfire?

12 MANAGING

Meanwhile, back at Keith's . . .

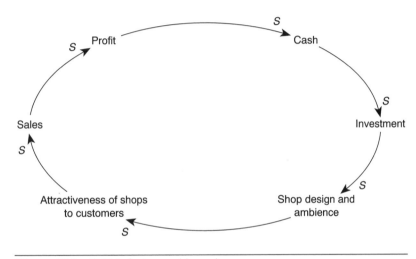

Figure 12.1 Keith's first causal loop diagram

'Yes,' continued Sam, 'I agree with you, Keith: that would be a lovely problem to have – it's the dream of every business to grow for ever. But we all know that it just can't be true. In the short term, yes, our business can grow exponentially, fuelled by the reinforcing loop you just drew on the flipchart. That loop captures my mental model really well, and it's great to feel that we all see things in the same way. But that reinforcing loop just can't be the whole picture. To me, it's the core but, sooner or later, exponential growth must slow down – some constraint must bite.'

'I'm sure you're right there, Sam,' added Paul. 'I've been thinking about that too. And I'm reminded of what I experienced when I visited our shop in Canterbury a few weeks ago. It's a lovely shop, in one of the best positions possible, nearly opposite the Cathedral Gate. But when I went there, it was terribly overcrowded – I think that several tourist buses must have just disgorged their entire contents. To me, that influences the link between "Shop design and ambience" and "Attractiveness of shops to customers". I believe that the link you've shown is right, Keith, but I wonder if there's another link too. The shop design and ambience certainly does attract people in, but it also causes overcrowding, congestion and queues. That could be a turn-off too.'

'Is this the sort of thing you have in mind?' asked Keith, turning once more to the flipchart.

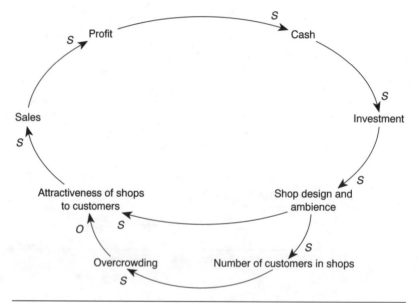

Figure 12.2 The introduction of a second, balancing loop, capturing the effect of overcrowding

'Yes,' replied Paul, 'it is. As we improve our shop design, we encourage a greater number of customers into our shops, so that's an *S*. And as the number of people in any shop increases, this sooner or later causes overcrowding, so that's another *S*. But as the shop becomes increasingly overcrowded, the overall attractiveness of the shop to other customers goes down no matter how well designed the shop is. That explains the *O*, doesn't it?'

'That makes sense to me,' continued Martin. 'It's the classic tourist hideaway problem: hideaways are very appealing, so long as no-one else chooses to hide away there too!'

'What we've done,' said Sam, 'is to add a balancing loop on the bottom of the original growth loop. And the effect of that must be to brake the exponential spinning of the reinforcing loop. Yes. I see it. The growth loop spins away to start with, and goes round several times before the number of people in the shops hits the kind of level that makes it unattractive for more people to come in. This dampens down the growth until it hits some sort of equilibrium.'

'Mmm,' said Martin. 'I wonder. Maybe it causes some kind of oscillation. You can imagine it. It's Saturday morning, the shop gets crowded and passers-by don't bother to go in. Then, as you approach lunchtime, the original crowds go away, the shop looks emptier, people are attracted back in and so on.'

'Like queues at supermarket checkouts,' added Keith. 'They behave a bit like that too.'

'That's right,' continued Sam. 'But the situation we really must avoid is to cause so much overcrowding that we discourage people from ever coming in. That would cause the reinforcing loop to flip into vicious mode, and we'd be in deep trouble then.'

'And that,' said Keith, 'is *not* a nice problem to have!'

'While we're on the subject of bad news, Keith,' said Paul, 'Can I add a further feature? Something else happens when the number of customers attracted to our shops increases. Any shop has only a finite catchment area and, as the number of people we attract increases, we are, by definition, attracting a greater and greater proportion of the local population in. This must saturate the market in at least two ways. Certainly, it's crazy to expect the entire population of Canterbury to want to visit our local shop – our total target market is only a proportion of the local population anyway and, for all we know, they might all be regular customers by now. And as we attract a wider cross-section of people in, their tastes become more diverse, and so they buy less of the merchandise we have on display, so the average purchase size goes down.'

'Hang on a second, Paul,' interrupted Keith, 'you're going like a steam train. Let me try to capture what you're saying. If I understand you correctly, what you're suggesting is that an increase in the number of customers visiting the shops has at least two additional effects. One is to increase market share, which must be constrained by the size of the total market; the second is to decrease the average spend per customer.'

'Yes, that's about right,' agreed Paul.

'Let me see if I can capture those two ideas,' continued Keith, 'but I'll probably need to redraw the original diagram. That'll take a moment or two. Why don't we take a break, get some coffees and reconvene in about five minutes?'

Managing growth

While Keith and his team take their break, let's reflect on the continuation of their conversation.

In Chapter 10, we reached a point in which Keith had just drawn the causal loop diagram originally shown as Figure 10.1 and reproduced in Figure 12.1. This is a familiar reinforcing loop, which captures the mental models of Keith and his colleagues. It implies unlimited exponential growth which the team rightly recognizes cannot go on for ever, and so they begin to examine the likely constraints. Paul then suggests the problem of overcrowding, which led to the drawing of Figure 12.2, in which the original reinforcing loop is combined with a balancing loop.

This combination of a reinforcing loop with a balancing loop is another very common structure, and is referred to as the *limits to growth* archetype. The usual behaviour of such a structure is an initial period of growth, fuelled by the reinforcing loop. Then, at some point during the growth phase, the action of the balancing loop becomes increasingly powerful, and the negative feedback from the O component puts the brakes on. What happens next depends on how hard the brakes come on, and the specifics of the time lags through the two loops. Sometimes the growth smooths off to a steady state in which the growth dynamic of the reinforcing loop is exactly counterbalanced by the braking effect of the balancing loop; sometimes the system oscillates as periods of growth occur in between periods of decline; sometimes the brakes bite so hard that the original growth trend is thrown into exponential and terminal decline.

We've all seen each of these three behaviours in business: businesses that grow to a steady state and remain unchanged for a while; businesses that seem continuously to be in the throes of boom and bust; businesses that boom and then bust, just the once. These are all symptomatic of limits to growth structures in which a reinforcing loop (we must spend more on advertising) is fighting against some constraint (but people are just no longer interested in the product).

Needless to say, as the story of Keith and his colleagues hints, life is never so simple as one reinforcing loop interacting with one balancing loop. In reality, most businesses represent a reinforcing loop – driven, ultimately, by the energy of managers – battling against a whole series of nested balancing loops, all of which represent layers upon layers of constraints that stop the business from growing. In our story, we saw that the first plausible constraint was overcrowding in the shops but, towards the end of the conversation, Paul is speaking of the further constraint of the local catchment area. He is right. Once the issue of shop overcrowding is resolved, sooner or later the constraint of the local market size will bite and, once that is solved, something else will come into play.

The problem of growing a business, then, is a question of how best to manage a reinforcing loop through a minefield of successive balancing loops, each one representing a different constraint. Some of these constraints are external – the overall size of the market, for example – but many are internal – how many business have failed not because of external problems, such as the markets or the competition, but because of lethal self-inflicted wounds, such as the inability to communicate, train staff, recruit enough people consistent with the business dynamics or, quite simply, the failure to manage the process of growth itself?

To manage business growth successfully, you must steer your way through the successive layers of constraining balancing loops. Usually, these constraints reveal themselves in sequence – as soon as one is resolved, the next one begins to take effect. To steer your way through, not only must you find ways of dealing with the most immediate constraint without causing wild oscillations or terminal decline, but you must also look through the current problem to see the next few coming. Then you might be able to determine strategies, policies and tactics to manage those constraints before they bite. But, because this takes time, you need some foresight. Or else you will end up like the frogs.

Keith's new diagram

'Thanks for coming back so promptly,' said Keith as the others returned to the conference room. 'While you've been out, I've redrawn the causal loop diagram to capture my understanding of Paul's mental models concerning the size of the local catchment area, and the concept of average spend per customer.'

'Mmm,' said Sam, screwing up her eyes as she looked at the new diagram. 'Could you explain that, please?'

'Sure,' replied Keith. 'This new diagram is quite a bit more complicated. The new major concept that I've introduced is that of the 'customer base' towards the bottom of the diagram. My mental model here is that, in any given area, there are people

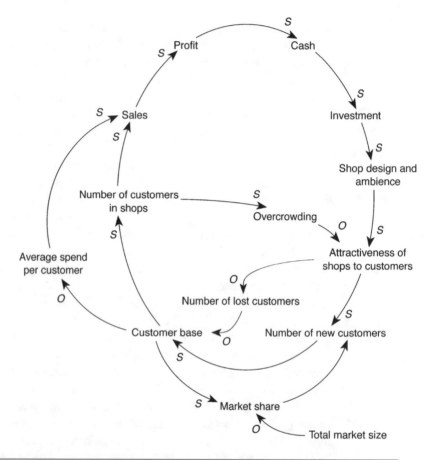

Figure 12.3 Keith's next causal loop diagram

who enjoy coming into our shops and will do so again and again. They're our loyal customers. But you wouldn't expect all our loyal customers to be in the shop all the time: they only visit when they need to or want to. But you would expect that the larger our customer base, the more people would be in the shops at any given time, hence the *S* between "Customer base" and "Number of customers in shops".'

'I follow that, and the idea of an overall customer base makes sense,' said Martin. 'But you said that your idea of the customer base related to our loyal customers who give us our repeat business. What is that item "Number of new customers"?'

'The issue there, Martin,' replied Keith, 'is driven by the question "Where does our customer base come from?". The item I have called "Number of new customers" represents those people who are attracted into the shop for the first time, primarily as a result of our shop design and ambience, and the overall attractiveness of the environment. The more attractive our shops, the greater the number of new customers – hence the *S* there – and the greater the number of new customers, the greater the established customer base, giving an *S* again.'

'That makes sense to me,' said Paul, nodding, 'and I can now see how those new items at the bottom of the diagram fit in. As the customer base grows, our market share gets bigger, so there is an *S* there but, as this happens, we increasingly saturate our natural market, and so the larger the market share, the harder it is to attract new customers. So that means there is an *O* linking "Market share" to "Number of new customers".'

'That's right,' continued Keith. 'And that *O* means that the loop from "Customer base" through "Market share" to "Number of new customers" and back to "Customer base" again is a balancing loop, limiting growth as our market share increases. That's how the constraint that Paul talked about before the break bites: sooner or later, the catchment area saturates.'

'Wait a minute, though,' interjected Paul, looking puzzled. 'When I look at that part of the diagram, I can see two *O*s: one linking "Total market size" to "Market share" and the other linking "Market share" to "Number of new customers". How can that be a balancing loop? I thought balancing loops were defined by having an odd number of *O*s.'

'You're right, Paul,' replied Keith. 'Balancing loops do have an odd number of *O*s – inside the loop, that is. If you look at the loop itself, you'll see just that – only one *O* connecting "Market share" to "Number of new customers". The other *O* is actually outside the loop itself – it connects "Total market size" to "Market share", and it happens to be an *O* simply because the definition of market share has total market size on the bottom of a division sum: for any given customer base, as the total market size goes up, the market share must go down. But "Market share" is a dangle – an item not fully connected into a feedback loop of its own, but acting as a target or limit on a balancing loop. That's where the overall constraint comes from.'

'Let me see if I can follow all of that through,' said Sam thoughtfully. 'Our initial investment creates an attractive environment which draws new customers into the customer base. They enjoy their shopping experience, spend money, giving us our profits which we reinvest, attracting more new customers and so on. But as that goes on, our market share increases, and the pool of people who could potentially become new customers gradually dries up. That's how the original growth loop becomes constrained.'

'That's exactly right,' said Keith.

'What about that item on the left, "Average spend per customer"?' asked Sam after a brief general silence.

'Oh yes. That's another new feature,' replied Keith. 'Do you remember, before the break, Paul suggested that, as the customer base becomes more diverse, the average spend per customer is likely to go down? I've captured that by linking "Customer base" to "Average spend per customer" with an *O*. "Sales" can then be represented in terms of "Average spend per customer" and "Number of customers in shops".'

'And what about the new part in the middle, around the item "Number of lost customers"? That's new too,' observed Paul.

'Yes, it is,' said Keith. 'I introduced that to capture our mental model about overcrowding. It struck me that the fundamental effect of overcrowding is to cause us to lose customers – either by discouraging existing customers from returning or by deterring customers from coming into our shops in the first place. Either way, the greater the "Number of lost customers", the smaller the "Customer base", hence the *O*.'

'So,' ventured Sam, 'your idea is that as the "Number of customers in shops" increases, this increases the "Overcrowding", which diminishes the "Attractiveness of shops to customers", hence the *O* there. Then – wait a moment – oh yes, as the "Attractiveness of shops to customers" *de*creases, this *in*creases the "Number of lost customers", so that's another *O*.'

'Yes, Sam, you've got it,' affirmed Keith. 'And when you add the last link from "Number of lost customers" back to "Customer base", there are now three *O*s in that feedback loop. An odd number of *O*s implies a balancing loop, so now we have yet another constraint on growth – a constraint attributable to overcrowding.'

'Mmm,' said Paul rubbing his chin. 'That diagram really is quite a bit more complicated than the original one of just a single reinforcing loop. But although it appears to be complicated, it really is quite intelligible. What we've done is to make the original diagram of a single reinforcing loop more realistic by adding three balancing loops – the one you explained just now to capture the concept of overcrowding, the one which recognizes the decreasing average spend per customer, and the third which is limited by the local market size. Our engine of growth is therefore constrained by three limits – overcrowding, spending and the total market. That makes sense to me, but I wonder if there are any more?'

The meeting fell silent as everyone looked at Keith's new diagram, thinking about Paul's question.

'You know, Keith,' said Martin. 'I suspect Paul has a point, but I'm still a bit worried about the right hand side there. It all looks a bit too complicated and cluttered to me. I can appreciate that the concepts of "Shop design and ambience" and "Attractiveness of shops to customers" are rather different – design, for example, is determined by us and is under our control, whereas attractiveness is a perception on the part of our customers. But we introduced those concepts at the start of the workshop before we got into what seems to me to be the fundamental issue of what drives the customer base. I wonder if we can simplify matters by replacing "Attractiveness of shops to customers" and "Shop design and ambience" by something else?'

'What do you have in mind?' asked Keith.

'I'm not quite sure,' replied Martin. 'Something like "Quality of shopping experience" keeps buzzing round in my head. I know that "quality" is a much overused term and can sometimes be a bit vague but, in this context, it seems to me to capture everything we're talking about. Isn't that the real reason why customers come back? And isn't it fundamental to attracting new customers too? It's also something we care about and can encompass factors such as design, ambience, customer service, merchandise – the lot. Let me show you what I mean.'

Taking the felt-tip pen, Martin drew a new diagram on a fresh sheet of flipchart paper.

'This diagram is very similar to the last one,' explained Martin, 'but I just feel it's that bit less cluttered. What do you think?'

Learning

PAUSE FOR THOUGHT

What do you think?

Examine Figure 12.4, which is a much more complex causal loop diagram than any we have seen before. Is it meaningful? Can you see how the different loops interact? Is it too complicated? Or is it really quite a powerful expression of some of the key features of what is in fact a very complex real situation – the growth dynamic of a retail business?

While Keith and his team consider Figure 12.4, let us, too, reflect for a moment. No-one could pretend that Figure 12.4 is simple. It isn't. But then neither is real life. And, as you'll recall from the elephant story, our quest has been for a meaningful representation of complexity: a representation which appreciates the contribution of each of the component parts but maintains their interconnectedness – a representation which embraces the complexity but renders it intelligible.

You are now in a position to judge, for Figure 12.4 takes us closer to the end of our journey: a journey which started with the stories of the elephant and the wine; that brought us to the idea of feedback loops; that introduced the concept of mental models; that showed us the two fundamental building blocks of the reinforcing loop and the balancing loop; that enabled us to compile the diagram of Figure 12.4 – a complex intertwining of one reinforcing loop with three balancing loops.

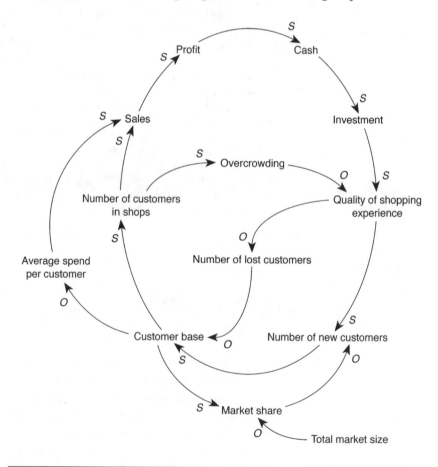

Figure 12.4 Martin's final causal loop diagram

The process by which Keith and his team arrived at the diagram of Figure 12.4 demonstrated several important features.

First, it started simple. The original diagram of Figure 10.1 was simple – simplistic even – but it was a very valuable starting point, particularly in the way in which it facilitated the sharing of the underlying individual mental models, and the building of consensus. As the discussion continued, the diagram became progressively enriched and more complex but also a better representation of reality. By increasing the complexity of the original diagram in stages, the team were better able to grapple with the increasing complexity and to continue to validate it against their mental models. And as this process developed, the structure of the diagram changed, resulting ultimately in the replacement of two of the concepts that were considered to be fundamental to the original diagram – 'Shop design and ambience' and 'Attractiveness of shops to customers' – by the single concept 'Quality of shopping experience'.

Does this imply that the original diagram was wrong, and that the original concepts were flawed? By no means. The original diagram was not 'wrong', and the concepts are quite valid. But, as we saw many chapters ago, while a problem is being solved the current state of the answer is inevitably 'wrong' – or, perhaps more accurately, 'incomplete'. And here we have yet another example of this fundamental truth. Any causal loop diagram is a representation of a set of mental models associated with an issue of interest and represents the current solution to the problem expressed by the question 'How can we gain an insight into a real, complex issue?'. In this sense, no causal loop diagram can ever be 'right'; rather, any causal loop diagram is merely a representation of our current state of thinking, and this will necessarily evolve as we think harder and deeper. So expect causal loop diagrams to change their content and the pattern of their relationships; do not cast them in concrete.

During this process people think about the issues, examine their mental models and compare these against other people's. The causal loop diagram provides a focus of attention, and the nature of the discussion among the team members demonstrates an active and safe process of articulation and challenge. And, during this process, as people think and listen, their mental models evolve. Is there another term for this? How, then, would you define learning? Not rote learning, as we discussed towards the end of Chapter 10, but learning in the far deeper sense of grappling with the complexity of real problems, of gaining a better understanding of what colleagues believe and think, of recognizing that there may be parts of the elephant that you have never appreciated, let alone thought about.

Policy

'I think that diagram makes a lot of sense,' said Sam, after several minutes' thought. 'I don't think I would have come up with it myself, and if I had just been presented with the whole diagram cold, I would never have understood it. But the way we built it up, step-by-step, makes it come alive.'

'I agree,' said Paul. 'It's a far cry from the simple reinforcing loop we started with, but it's much more realistic.'

'I follow it,' said Martin, 'but I have a real problem with understanding how it behaves. When we had just a single reinforcing loop, I could see how it grew exponentially and, although in the long term that had to be unrealistic, at least I had an intuitive feel for what was going on. And when we added the first balancing item – "Overcrowding" I think it was – I could see how that limited the exponential growth. But now I don't have a clue. Does that structure grow? Oscillate? Spiral? How on earth can you tell?'

'That's a very valid point,' agreed Keith. 'As soon as a few loops start acting together, I find it impossible to grasp how the behaviour will evolve.'

'We could always simulate the dynamic behaviour on a computer model,' said Sam. 'There are several packages that can do that, and one I know is called 'ithink'. But my experience with computer modelling is that, although it can be a very valuable technique in helping quantify the effects of various assumptions, a lot of insight can be gained without the need for simulation simply by studying the causal loop diagram. In our case, for example, I don't think our issue here is to determine in numerical terms how fast our business can grow, or how long it will take to reach a given level of profit, or specifically how much to invest on carpets or whatever. Sure, I understand that we need answers to questions like that from time to time, but I think the issues before us now are not so much numeric as generic. How can we stimulate and manage growth? How can we manage around the constraints? Where are the constraints? In what sequence will they bite? What ideas can we generate to get round the various problems? These are policy matters. And to me they're underpinned by insight, not by numbers.'

'Following that line of thought,' continued Keith, 'what do we think are the major constraints we face? Have we captured them on the diagram? Or are any missing?'

There was a silence as the group studied the diagram.

'I can't think of anything missing from the diagram right now,' said Martin eventually, 'but the key to me seems to be the issue of growing and maintaining the customer base. The more we can encourage people to come to our shops again and again, the more resilient we are to the limiting effect of the overall size of the market.'

'What can we do, then, to maximize the level of repeat business?' asked Keith.

'Clearly, as the diagram says, we need to ensure the quality of what we offer. And that implies all sorts of things – high quality merchandise, shop design and ambience as we discussed earlier, well-trained and courteous staff. All those sorts of things,' replied Martin.

'I wonder,' said Sam brightly. 'The diagram triggers some new thoughts. Repeat business is not just about the quality of the experience, but also about loyalty. What could we do to improve customer loyalty or build stronger relationships?'

'Do you mean things like mailshots, coupons, discounts to regular customers, customer loyalty programmes, that sort of thing?' asked Paul.

'I guess so,' replied Sam. 'I haven't really thought it through.'

'Those are good ideas,' said Keith. 'Do you think it would be worthwhile to convene another workshop specifically to explore some ideas for addressing these sorts of issues?'

'I do,' replied Paul. 'And, as well as addressing the question of how to maximize repeat business, I'd add "How to attract new customers" and "How to increase average spend per customer".'

'Sounds good to me,' agreed Sam.

'Me too,' said Martin.

'Well,' said Keith, 'that seems to be a good conclusion to a very productive workshop. I'll circulate some copies of all the causal loop diagrams and draft a brief summary of the supporting mental models. I'm very pleased we have a shared understanding of what we collectively believe makes our business grow, and we have homed in on three key topics: how to maintain the base of loyal, repeat customers; how best to attract new customers; and how to increase the average spend per customer. It strikes me that there's a lot of scope for innovation in each of those. So, thank you, everybody, for a lively session. We'll continue next week.'

And so, back to innovation

At last. We're back to innovation. Did you see how?

It happened at two levels. One level was by studying the causal loop diagram, which enabled people to focus on particular areas, especially the constraints that were potentially holding growth back. As a general rule, when you are pushing against a constraint, you have two choices of strategy. One is to push harder and see what happens. This is usually under your control, since it is you who does the pushing. So, with a declining market share, you might choose to spend more money on advertising. In business, however, the constraints are often (but by no means always) external, and they are much bigger than you are. So when you push hard, the constraint pushes back, but much, much harder.

The alternative strategy is to alleviate the constraint. So instead of throwing money at advertising a terminally ill product, you invest in product development. This requires you to understand more about the constraint and how and where it operates, and, if the constraint is external, you may seem to have less, rather than more, control. More significantly, because examining and easing constraints can be more costly and time-consuming than pushing harder, shortsighted macho managers often favour the short-term apparent quick win of the heroic push. Smarter longer-sighted managers usually spot that it is far less tiring to release the brake than to go on pedalling like crazy.

As you can see from the story, systems thinking encouraged the team to explore the whereabouts of the constraints and led to a natural discussion about how to relieve them. This is because systems thinking demands a holistic view in which constraints are recognized as an integral part of the problem. Constraints are also usually on the boundaries, and this is another example of where to look for opportunities for innovation, as we saw in Chapter 5.

The second level is that of the mental model. Throughout the discussion of the 'How do we grow?' question, mental models were being articulated, explained, interrogated, challenged and modified. But what is a mental model? Yes, as we have already seen, it is a statement of belief, of a deeply held assumption, a cherished sacred cow. But is it not also the fundamental basis of innovation – the equivalent of your Beethoven symphony, your Steinbeck novel? The fundamental structure that needs to be exposed, challenged and disaggregated to support innovation?

And isn't that exactly what you could see happening in the story?

13 KNOWLEDGE

Descartes was wrong

The year is 1631; the place, Paris – the Paris of the aloof King Louis XIII, of his beautiful wife Anne of Austria and of the mysterious Armand-Jean du Plessis, Cardinal de Richelieu. In the streets, the Cardinal's elegant guards swagger, basking in the glory of their master's power; in the taverns, the King's moustachioed musketeers swap stories of military and romantic conquest.

In one such tavern, in a small room above the parlour – a room badly lit and drowned in the noise of construction work at the nearby Louvre – the 35-year-old René Descartes is being interviewed for a job.

'You have a very impressive CV, Monsieur Descartes,' said the senior interviewer, nodding his head.

'Yes,' chimed in his number two, 'you're obviously quite a thinker.'

'Thank you,' responded Descartes, casting his eyes down modestly.

'Tell me, monsieur,' continued the interlocutor. 'What do you think is the most important quality you bring?'

'Well,' replied Descartes, animatedly, 'I've thought about that a lot. Yes, a lot. I don't want to appear arrogant, but I really do believe I have quite a powerful mind. I like solving problems. I like thinking. And I think I'm a very good thinker.'

'Really? Tell us some more. Give us some examples, please.'

'Thank you for asking. I had a good thought the other day. I haven't written it down yet – maybe I'll get round to writing a book sometime, but I just seem to be too busy right now. Anyway, my thought. Yes. It was "*Cogito, ergo sum; je pense, donc je suis*, I think, therefore I am".'

'I think, therefore I am?'

'Yes, that's right. "I think, therefore I am".'

'And how, Monsieur Descartes, how does such an egocentric statement as "*I* think, therefore *I* am" equip you to be a team player? Hm?'

'Well, er . . . I'm not sure . . .'

Poor Descartes. He didn't get the job. Clearly, Descartes was a very intelligent man, but was he a team player? The interviewers, presumably, thought not, and what organization wants to recruit individualists, loners? Surely everyone needs to be a good team player, bonded, and loyal?

But what is a team? Is it merely any group of individuals that happen to be in the same place at the same time? And if all the members of that group happen to work for the same large organization, surely they must be a team, because we're all team players, aren't we?

Or is a team a much more subtle concept? How do teams behave? Can individuals be excluded from a team, or not invited to join one? Or is such an action the antithesis of teamwork?

These were some of the questions posed at the beginning of Chapter 8, before we embarked on our journey into the rich worlds of systems thinking. And these are the questions to which we return in this, the final, chapter. Teamwork is, of course, an extremely well studied subject, and if there is one theme on which the many books on the subject agree, it is that teamwork is a very complex topic. But since one of the themes of this book is that the intrinsic complexity of a problem should not act as a deterrent to its exploration, I trust that the thoughts expressed on the following few pages will contribute constructively to the debate.

My starting point is to return to Descartes. '*Cogito, ergo sum: je pense, donc je suis*', 'I think, therefore I am.' The problem with this statement is that it refers to 'I'. It is, as the interviewer observed, totally egocentric. It lacks the concept of the team – of 'we', of 'us'.

So how can you get the concept of the team, of 'we', of 'us', into '*Cogito, ergo sum*'? What happens when you put 'us' into '*Cogito, ergo sum*'?

I think, therefore we are

If you put 'us' into '*Cogito, ergo sum*', you get '*Cogito, ergo sum*-us'. '*Cogito, ergo sumus*'. In Latin, *sumus* means 'we are'. Mmmm. '*Cogito, ergo sumus: je pense, donc nous sommes*'; '*I think, therefore we are*'.

Now there's a thought – a thought that embraces teamwork. Because 'I think', therefore 'we are': my contribution helps us all to succeed; what I do adds to what you do, and what you do adds to what I do. Teamwork. Knowledge. Sharing. Try this 'Pause for thought'.

PAUSE FOR THOUGHT

What is the difference between you, acting by yourself, and you, acting as part of a team?

You can answer that only for yourself, drawing on your own experience. My answer necessarily draws on my own experience, so let me share my thoughts here.

For much of my career, I have acted as a management consultant in large professional partnerships, in an environment populated by highly motivated, extremely talented people. Each one of us is more than capable of earning a living by ourselves as sole traders. So what are the benefits of staying within a professional partnership? I suggest that there are two main ones. The first is the association of the individual with a brand. Because the firm has a brand name which transcends the reputation of the individual, but which has of course been built up by the collective achievement of many individuals over decades, the role of the individual is subsumed within the image of the brand and this gives the individual an immediate cachet. This is of great benefit to the individual, for it solves the individual's marketing problem – unless you are one of the very few true management gurus, it is far easier to win business as part of a well known firm than as an individual. There is also a corresponding benefit to the client: from the client's point of view, contracting with a firm, rather than an individual, reduces risk.

There is, in addition, a second benefit. In consultancy, the client is purchasing a package of services – an independent sounding-board, access to short-term resources to get things done, access to knowledge and know-how. As a sole trader, with a few associates, it is possible to deliver all these benefits – the sole trader can be the sounding board and has his or her own knowledge and, through associates and agencies, can also deploy short-term resources. But, as a partner in a large firm, the opportunity to add value is – potentially – vastly greater. By being part of a team or a firm, the partner has ready access not only to an extensive resource pool of very varied and high calibre skills but, far, far more importantly, to the knowledge and experience of others not only within the firm, but through them to the firm's clients. Any client can therefore gain benefit not solely from the personal knowledge and experience of their immediate consultants but, potentially, from the knowledge and experience of everyone else in the firm. The ability to form and effectively deploy a knowledge network is one of the very few examples whereby scale can bring true benefit to a professional service: the greater the number of people who contribute to the knowledge pool, the greater the benefit of that collective knowledge to each individual.

To me, the difference between me as a sole trader and me as a member of a team boils down to two key themes. The first is *cohesive action*. Because we are a team, we have a higher level of mutual trust, respect and empathy than a random group, and so we can act more effectively, consistently and cohesively. The second is *coherent knowledge*. Because we are a team, we can more effectively share and deploy our mutual knowledge to both our own and our clients' benefit. We can form a 'knowledge pool' – a 'brain bank'. *Cogito, ergo sumus. Je pense, donc nous sommes.* I think, therefore we are.

CASE FILE

The power of knowledge

Some time ago, one of my assignments was to carry out a feasibility study for ways of improving the capture, transfer and use of knowledge in a particular organization. When drafting the final report, one of my colleagues suggested

that we write a management summary which encapsulated the heart of the issue. His suggestion was a single sentence:

In this organization today, knowledge is a source of internal competitive advantage.

My colleague was profoundly perceptive for, in that organization, the possession of knowledge by any one individual was an opportunity for that individual to score points off everyone else.

'*Cogito, ergo sum*' indeed.

Cohesive action

What would you cite as the most impressive examples of teamwork?

Most people respond to that question by reference to sport or the military, so let's take sport as our first example.

SPORT

We are all thrilled to see the displays of supremely skilled cohesive action when two great sporting teams meet, especially in fast-moving games such as football, rugby and ice-hockey. Although individuals may be stars, in the greatest teams, their personal agendas are subordinated to those of the team, and we marvel at how the players anticipate the play and position themselves in exactly the right place to receive the pass. To me, there are three key themes on display here:

- All the players have a similarly high level of personal skill.
- All the players are sincerely committed to a genuinely shared objective.
- The players anticipate each other's actions with very few direct orders.

These themes also apply in a management context. The first concerns technical skill, and my experience is that members of high-performing management teams each hold all the other members in high esteem – an esteem earned by the contribution each team member is seen to be making. Surely no group can be called a team if its members bad-mouth each other, either in public, or worse, in private. Although the skills brought by each team member might, and usually are, different from a technical standpoint, if each individual shows what Peter Senge calls 'personal mastery', then each can make a valuable, and valued, contribution. This does not imply that, in business, all team members must have equal levels of skill and experience; rather, that the skill demonstrated by each team member is regarded by all others as excellent in the context of the individual's experience and in relation to the task at hand.

The second theme is about commitment to a shared objective. In sport, the shared objective is usually very explicit but, even in the context of the extremely clear objective of scoring more goals than the other side, we have all seen examples of individual players who place their own vainglory above the team's collective objective and fail to pass the ball to another player who is facing an open goal.

In business the objectives are often less clear, and the personal and political agendas of individuals loom more significant. But in the absence of a truly shared commitment to the same objective, a group can never be a team, for the individuals will surely fall out when something goes wrong. How often have you witnessed someone's joy when another is seen to fail? How often have you seen so-called colleagues distance themselves from an unfortunate person who is encountering real problems?

To me, the most important aspect of commitment is that no individual can enforce their personal commitment on anybody else. Commitment can only be given voluntarily. So, building commitment to a truly shared objective – building a team – can occur only if the individuals wish it to happen. And this is why mental models are so fundamentally important. My mental models reflect my deeply held beliefs. If I find that my mental models naturally overlap with someone else's, this discovery forms a bridge to deeper mutual understanding and teamwork; if, on the other hand, I discover that my mental models are quite different from someone else's, yes, I can work with that person, but the likelihood of building a truly shared commitment to anything but relatively trivial goals is low.

The spontaneous and natural sharing of mental models is, to me, a necessary condition for building a high-performing team. But since we rarely articulate our mental models explicitly, it takes time for the individuals in a group to discover what mental models each individual holds, and the extent to which they are naturally shared. That's why systems thinking can be so powerful and beneficial. As we have seen, systems thinking provides a natural, safe and well-focused method that enables mental models to be declared and exposed. And, since systems thinking is also a very powerful technique for taming complexity, for seeing problems in the whole and for teasing out chains of causality, it is also a very practical way of tackling even the most difficult business problems.

During this process, the mental models held by each individual can be expressed, and compared with those of others. As a result, not only do the members of the group gain a deeper understanding of each other, but each individual – if he or she is willing to let it happen – has the opportunity to extend his or her own mental models; to learn; to change the boundaries of his or her mind; to innovate at the most fundamental level. And through this process of expressing their own mental models, of listening to those of others, of extending their own mental models, they may choose, voluntarily, to give their commitment. When this happens to all the members of a group, they are transformed from a mere group of individuals into a team – a team with a deeply shared commitment.

One of the most significant results of building commitment at this level is that individuals become far more adept at anticipating how others are behaving and how others would react in a given situation. On the football field, this manifests itself in the striker who miraculously moves into a position to take the long pass from midfield; in business, by the trust and respect gained by knowing that, had you been faced with that decision, you would have chosen exactly the same path as your team colleague.

This anticipatory empathy, this high level of trust and respect, can very easily be recognized. On the football field, for example, the midfielder did not send a memo to the striker to instruct him to be in such-and-such a position in four seconds' time – it happened naturally, by empathy, without formal communication.

Furthermore, in a high-performing team, roles can often be fluid, with different people taking the role of leader at different times. By the same token, different people take the role of follower at different times, without feeling anxious about losing their previous leadership position. High-performing teams have not only able leaders, but also willing followers.

CASE FILE

How to identify teams

Another of my assignments was to help a professional firm create a new organization structure. The firm was growing fast, and there were several suggestions for the way the teams should be organized – for example, by geographical location, by technical skill, or by market sector.

There was, however, another – by natural friendship groups.

The client had a voice-mail messaging system and, with everyone's permission, we

'tapped' the system over a period of time not to snoop on the messages, but to identify who regularly communicated with whom. We found that there were two patterns: one was the pattern of necessary business communication, but the other was the pattern of voluntary conversation, of people communicating with each other not because they had to, but because they wanted to.

This second pattern identified networks of individuals who actively sought each other out – networks of naturally

forming teams. These natural clusters formed the basis of the new organization where, within each cluster, there was a high level of trust, respect and teamwork, transcending geography, technical skill and market sector.

True, the teamwork between the clusters was not so good, but everyone agreed that an organization based on natural teams was far more effective than one formed from artificial 'teams' created by forcing together people who just did not get on.

THE MILITARY

Or, to be precise, the Navy.

Britain's greatest naval commander is acknowledged to be Horatio Nelson, the victor of Trafalgar. But why was he great?

Most people would say that Nelson was great because he was daring and had great courage. Naval historians, however, would say something different: Nelson was indeed daring and had supreme courage but, primarily, he was great because he made others great. Nelson was a master coach, and he was victorious at Trafalgar not solely because of his own prowess, but rather because of the skills he had built in his captains and the corresponding trust that he placed in them.

There are two wonderful anecdotes that support this.

The first is that of a meeting held in 1805, the year of the Battle of Trafalgar, between Nelson and Lord Barham, the first Lord of the Admiralty. Lord Barham handed Nelson a list of the naval officers of the time and invited him to select his own team. 'Choose yourself, my Lord,' replied Nelson. 'The same spirit actuates the whole profession. You cannot choose wrong.'

What businessman, when invited to choose his own team for a particular task or project, could say the same when given the internal telephone directory?

The second anecdote has a very modern implication. It concerns the conduct of naval battles and the role of communications. In Nelson's time, the technology of communications consisted of hoisting combinations of three or four flags to the top of the mast, their meanings being defined in two standard code books, *The Signal Book for Ships of War*, first compiled in 1790, and the *Marine Vocabulary* of 1803. Some flag combinations referred to frequently used complete messages such as 'Engage the enemy ·more closely', others referred to individual words, while others enabled words to be spelt letter by letter. Given the necessarily limited number of precoded messages, this system was clumsy, time-consuming and potentially error-prone if ever a commander wished to send a signal that did not conform to some previously defined formula.

This is exactly what happened when, just before the Battle of Trafalgar, Nelson rallied his fleet with his famous signal 'England expects that every man will do his duty'.

In fact, this was not the signal that Nelson had wished to send. Nelson's original intention was to exhort his men with the more personal 'Nelson confides that every man will do his duty', which he instructed Lieutenant John Pasco to encode and send to the fleet. Pasco, however, informed Nelson that the words 'Nelson', 'confides' and 'duty' would all have to be spelt letter by letter, and that this would be very cumbersome under the circumstances. Pasco further suggested that the phrase 'Nelson confides' be replaced by 'England expects', which did conform to the code book standards, leaving only 'duty' to be spelt out. Nelson accepted his subordinate's advice, and Pasco duly transmitted the joint Nelson–Pasco wording with a signal of 32 flags.

As a commander, Nelson fully recognized the constraints imposed by the rudimentary technology of signalling available to him – constraints on both the efficiency of transmitting and receiving messages, as well as on the independence of behaviour allowed to his captains. Nelson therefore used signals only very sparingly and, when battle was engaged, hardly at all. As a consequence, Nelson did not command his captains, and control them: rather, he left them to their own initiative, satisfied in the knowledge that, because he had trained them, they would react to any given circumstances just as he himself would. He had built a community of truly shared knowledge, vision and mental models.

Do not suppose, however, that Nelson did not communicate at all. Far from it. His preferred method of communication was face-to-face. When his fleet was not in action, his captains were frequently in conference with him round the table in his flagship, listening, discussing, arguing, learning. That's how he built the coherent knowledge that led to the cohesive action they all demonstrated.

This anecdote does not end with Nelson. During the nineteenth century, communications technology was enhanced, and methods were devised to increase the repertoire of flag signals that could be communicated. The introduction of wireless transmission in the early twentieth century allowed even more sophisticated communication.

What do you think happened as a result of the improvements to communications technology?

Well, what happened was that admirals soon learnt that they could send much more explicit instructions to their captains, more easily, more securely and more frequently. And, by the same token, the captains learnt that they needn't, or indeed shouldn't, take action until instructed to do so. The effect of improving the communications technology was to build a command-and-control culture which deprived captains of all initiative – a command-and-control culture that nearly resulted in the destruction of the pride of the British Navy at the Battle of Jutland in 1916.

Intuitively, we might expect that an improvement in communications technology would result in improved teamwork. Perhaps so, but perhaps

CASE FILE

Same side, different teams

In the early stages of the Battle of Jutland in 1916, Vice-Admiral Sir David Beatty was leading the British battlecruiser fleet southwards towards the coast of Germany. Beatty's mission was to scout ahead of the full British Grand Fleet, led by Admiral Sir John Jellicoe.

During the late afternoon of 31 May, Beatty, in HMS *Lion*, with three other battlecruisers, was several miles ahead of four *Queen Elizabeth*-class battleships – the most modern and powerful battleships afloat – under the immediate command of Beatty's subordinate, Rear-Admiral Hugh Evan-Thomas. Evan-Thomas's flagship, HMS *Barham*, was named after that same Lord Barham whom we met in connection with Nelson's choice of officers – an irony indeed in view of what was about to happen.

At 4.40 pm Beatty made contact with the German High Seas Fleet, led by Vice-Admiral Reinhard Scheer in the *Friedrich der Grosse*, heading north. Beatty turned around, with the intention of luring the German Fleet towards Jellicoe.

At 4.46 pm, Beatty, heading north, approached Evan-Thomas, heading south, directly towards the Germans. It was not until 4.54 pm that Evan-Thomas instructed his ships to turn around, following an order from Beatty, the exact timing of which is a matter of dispute. Between 4.54 and 4.59 pm, Evan-Thomas's four ships, the pride of the Navy, followed one another through a 180° turn. But, by now, they had steamed within range of the German fleet. In the resulting bombardment 250 British sailors were killed or injured but, by great good fortune, no battleship was sunk.

For years afterwards, Beatty and Evan-Thomas bickered over who should take the blame. Beatty claimed that Evan-Thomas should have acted on his own initiative, turning his fleet as soon as Beatty came into sight. Evan-Thomas claimed that Beatty should have given him the order to turn sooner.

not. How often have you heard the argument that an organization's communication problems will be 'solved' by enhanced technology?

THE ORCHESTRA

Although sport and the military are the most commonly quoted examples of effective teamwork, to portray sportsmen or military leaders as the ideal role models leaves a bitter taste – in my mouth at any rate – because sport and the military are examples of a value I do not endorse: I win; you lose. Inevitably, in sport, and far more tragically in the military, when 'our' side shows great teamwork and wins, the 'enemy' necessarily loses.

How much better it would be to find an example of a high-performing team whose success does not rely on the failure of others. Fortunately for the human race, there is such an example – the symphony orchestra.

An orchestra is the ultimate high-performing team, participating in an activity in which everyone involved – the players, the audience, the conductor – wins. Each player, often possessing the skill (and perhaps temperament!) of a soloist, necessarily has to blend in with all the other players to create the performance which delights both the players as well as the audience. An orchestra usually also has a conductor, who does not blow the trumpets, who does not bang the drums. But when the same orchestra plays the same piece under different conductors, the performances are often significantly different, although the notes played are absolutely identical. Somehow, the conductor has imposed a meta-pattern over the basic pattern of the notes – a meta-pattern of shape and phrase, of emphasis and dynamic. A meta-pattern of his own. But how does a conductor do this? How does a conductor influence the players, so that, willingly, they play the music his way? And is this not a most powerful metaphor for management?

I suspect the response of Herbert von Karajan – for many years the charismatic and awesome conductor of the Berlin Philharmonic Orchestra – was 'fear'. Von Karajan was reputed to lead his orchestra with a rod of iron, and this is indeed one model of management. But there is another: a model espoused by Benjamin Zander, the conductor of the Boston Philharmonic – a model based on personal mastery, shared mental models, coaching, learning and empowerment.

Let us return for a moment to the three key attributes of teamwork, as noted during our discussion of sport:

- All the players have a similarly high level of personal skill.
- All the players are sincerely committed to a genuinely shared objective.
- The players anticipate each other's actions with very few direct orders.

In a symphony orchestra, the first point is self-evident: all the players must be equally expert. An orchestra cannot carry any technical passengers. The second point, the sharing of an objective, is central to Zander's approach, and he sees his role as a conductor very much as one of building a shared commitment to a unified performance. If, for example, the trombone drowns out the piccolo, that may be a boost to the trombonist's ego, but it may also damage the piece as a whole. So how do you persuade the trombonist to play quietly? The third point, that concerning anticipation and the absence of orders, is also evident, even when a conductor is present: how else could all the players of an orchestra – sometimes more than 100 individuals – act with such wonderful unity?

To build a high-performing team from individual players, Zander deploys a large repertoire of techniques, which he relates with great verve in his seminars and master classes. Let me describe just two of them here: how he builds confidence through recognition, and how he creates and shares a vision.

Zander knows all too well that musicians, like actors, thrive on recognition and applause. He therefore ensures that all the players are recognized in full not only after the performance by means of curtain calls, but also during rehearsals where he makes sure that even the most minor parts are explicitly recognized as contributing to the whole. During rehearsal, for example, Zander will often ask two different sets of musicians to play a few bars together, inviting the rest of the orchestra to listen and to provide feedback on the balance of the sound. This helps ensure that the different groups of musicians actively listen to one another, and that the intrinsically louder instruments don't drown out the softer ones. Zander is also lavish with praise, but not falsely so, for he fully appreciates that insincerity is corrosive.

Another mechanism of giving recognition is the technique Zander uses in his teaching role at the New England Conservatory of Music. At the start of his courses on performance, for example, he sees all the students individually to get to know them and to build rapport. He also says to them, 'For this course, I give you an "A" grade'. This invariably puzzles the students who point out that since the course has only just started, it is somewhat premature to declare the course grade. Zander then explains that his initial assumption is that he expects the student to attain an 'A' grade, and that he will do everything in his power to support the student in that endeavour. All that remains is for the student to demonstrate that he or she is indeed worthy.

Zander is convinced that, if you expect the best of people and support them, they will deliver the very best they can, and this is his method of declaring that conviction. In practice, he does not give everyone an 'A' grade, for he is not a soft touch. But by stating his assumption – his value set, his mental model – Zander believes that he encourages his students to perform, willingly, to the very limit of their abilities.

Let's turn now to vision – vision created by Zander's profoundly deep knowledge of every piece that he is to coach his orchestra to play. He studies the score intensively and always researches the history of the music itself. Zander's research has led to significant innovations in interpretation and performance, such as his playing of the end of the last movement of Shostakovitch's *Fifth Symphony* at a funereally slow pace, so that the effect of the brass behind the repeated notes of the strings, evoking a futile attempt to break through prison bars, is as heartrending an exposition of the struggle to be free from Stalinism as could be experienced by those, like us, who have not been subject to its tortures; such as his brisk speed for the *Alla Marcia* episode in the last movement of Beethoven's *Ninth Symphony*; such as the tempestuous tempo at which he takes the *Danse Sacrale* at the end of Stravinsky's *Rite of Spring*.

CASE FILE

The right *Rite*

When the *Rite of Spring* was first performed in Paris in 1913, the theatre exploded in uproar and a riot erupted in the streets. Never before had an audience experienced such dramatic, rhythmic, instinctive music.

In 1929, Stravinsky himself conducted a recording of the *Rite*, and, ever since, this has been regarded as the 'definitive' performance. That is, until Benjamin Zander discovered an old piano-roll of the *Rite* – a long tape of

perforated paper used as a program for a mechanical piano. The piano-roll is remarkable for the speed at which the last sequence, the *Danse Sacrale*, is played – the piano-roll being much, much faster than any recording. This last sequence portrays the sacrificial death of a young virgin, and Zander realized that the fast speed is far more appropriate than the slow one. He also discovered that the piano-roll was created by none other than Stravinsky himself – in 1920, nine years before his orchestral recording.

So why is Stravinsky's recording so slow? Zander suggests that Stravinsky wanted the recording to be fast, as on the piano-roll, but was unable to achieve this because his orchestra just couldn't do it. The technical limitations of his orchestra, therefore, obliged Stravinsky to make his recording at the slow speed.

Zander's live recording is at the fast speed – with an orchestra that includes amateur musicians. Empowered amateurs, that is.

Impassioned by his vision, Zander then imparts it to his orchestra, showing them how his vision creates a unified whole in which each individual musician has a vital role. To encourage the players to share in his vision, during rehearsals he distributes paper to each person, so that any ideas that may arise on phrasing, interpretation, balance, tempo or whatever can be noted and shared.

In Zander's lectures and workshops, he demonstrates how the conductor's vision can be shared using an immensely powerful demonstration. He asks his audience if there is anyone who has had a recent birthday. Even in a quite small group there always is. He invites that person to the front of the group, and then asks the rest of the group to sing *Happy Birthday*. Inevitably, everyone is embarrassed by this as few people – particularly smartly dressed businesspeople – relish singing *Happy Birthday* in public. But they are all in the same boat, so they all participate. Also, inevitably, the performance is somewhat lacklustre. Zander then suggests some ways of improving matters. In the first phrase, for example, where is the stress? Is it, for example, '*Happy* Birthday to you', 'Happy *Birthday* to you', or 'Happy Birthday to *you*'? Since the purpose of the song is to celebrate the individual, the group is likely to agree that the stress lies on *you* rather than on *happy* or *birthday*. Fine. So why not sing it with a significant stress on *you*? And they all sing it again with more feeling and much more articulate phrasing.

And so it goes on, until the group ends up singing *Happy Birthday* like they've never sung it before. But Zander hasn't finished yet. He asks them to sing one more time and, as they do, he walks away from the traditional position of the conductor at the front of the orchestra to a position on the side or at the back. The group continues to sing, without a conductor. It has voluntarily and willingly accepted his vision, and had been coached and empowered to deliver that vision even without direction.

No-one who has experienced singing *Happy Birthday* with Benjamin Zander will ever forget the experience of being coached into becoming a member of a high-performing team, even on the basis of limited technical skill.

Coherent knowledge

As we have seen, Nelson and Zander share the gift of being consummate coaches, sharing their knowledge with their teams and guiding, leading and empowering each individual team member to the topmost heights of team performance. The sharing of knowledge across a community is undoubtedly another fundamental attribute of high-performing teams, and it is to this topic to which I now turn.

Organizations inevitably accumulate, or at least encounter, vast quantities of knowledge. Over the years, some have developed extensive systems and procedures for the capture, archiving and retrieval of knowledge:

government departments, for example, keep enormous volumes of records; industrial firms keep details of product specifications; law firms store case precedents. Most people would agree that capturing, storing and facilitating the retrieval of knowledge is a 'good thing', and now that computer technology permits the building of colossal databases, this seems to be easier to accomplish than ever. All we have to do is tip everything into a huge database, and the problem is solved. But is it? I wonder.

HARD INFORMATION, SOFT KNOWLEDGE

My starting point is to distinguish between two categories of knowledge.

The first I call *hard information*, and this comprises material that is well defined, static and usually historic. Its specific nature will vary between organizations, but some examples include:

- minutes of meetings
- reports
- product blueprints and specifications
- marketing and sales brochures
- presentations
- externally sourced material such as press cuttings, third party reports and the rest.

The important characteristics of this type of knowledge concern the ability to identify titles, themes, topic and keywords, so facilitating indexing, cataloguing and subsequent retrieval. Good librarians or information officers are trained in the appropriate technical skills and also have the motivation to carry out the corresponding administrative procedures. Given a good librarian, sufficient storage space for documents, tapes, microfilm or whatever and reasonable disciplines to enable the information officers to collect the source material, then it is not difficult to organize and manage the archive.

There is, however, an additional important characteristic of this type of knowledge. It is static, in the sense that once the minutes have been taken, the report written or the blueprints signed off, the contents do not change. Archiving is therefore primarily a matter of indexing and storage: there is no requirement to update the material itself. The material itself may, of course, go out-of-date, in which case the originals stay in the archives gathering dust until some historian finds a reason to unearth them. The information content, however, remains unchanged.

My second category I call *soft knowledge*. This comprises material that, for the most part, is stored in people's heads: their personal knowledge, their memories, their judgements, their insights. In contrast to hard information, which is well defined and static, soft knowledge is ill-defined and dynamic: personal knowledge is very loosely structured and changes minute by minute. Furthermore, my soft knowledge is not limited to the contents of my own mind, for I also know something of the soft knowledge that is stored in the minds of others. Soft knowledge therefore exists within a complex network of personal interactions, as exemplified by the situation in which, when asked a question to which I do not know the answer, I might reply 'I'm sorry, I don't know. But I think Geoff knows quite a bit about that. Why don't you call him on . . .'. Invoking these interpersonal networks to distribute knowledge throughout organizations can be immensely powerful, for it provides the opportunity for the collective knowledge of the entire organization to be brought to bear whenever required. Wouldn't it be wonderful if we could somehow capture all the organization's soft knowledge and build a collective 'brain bank'?

Of course, in real life, it's not as easy as that, for there are often some very sturdy barriers.

The first barrier is the active and deliberate unwillingness of individuals to participate. I may indeed be aware of Geoff's ability to contribute some useful information, but I am not necessarily obliged to declare that fact. When asked the question 'Can you help?', the response 'Sorry, I just don't know' closes the matter down. Furthermore, since my interrogator need never find out that I knew Geoff might be able to help, I am safe. More extremely, I might be asked a question to which I *do* know the answer but, for all sorts of reasons, I might decide to pretend that I don't. This attitude of 'Why should my knowledge help him?' is, of course, the most direct manifestation of the '*Cogito, ergo sum*' syndrome discussed at the start of the chapter. Regrettably, it is the pervasive attitude in many organizations whose cultures therefore prevent the transfer of soft information across the organization as a whole, limiting it to transfers within non-interconnecting local networks of small groups and excluding lone individuals. The opportunity for those organizations to solve problems, to add value and to be effective is therefore enormously reduced. Their people may just as well be independent sole traders. Such cultural obstructionism is an enormous barrier.

There is, however, a second problem with the capture, storage, sharing and retrieval of soft knowledge – one that is not directly dependent on organizational culture. This concerns the nature of the knowledge content.

Clearly, any individual's personal knowledge base is entirely unique. But, independent of the specifics of that knowledge base, I believe it is possible to make some important generalizations.

PAUSE FOR THOUGHT

**Think for a moment about your own
knowledge base.**

How would you describe it?

First, any individual's knowledge base is vast. We all know very, very many things, and the concept of trapping all our personal knowledge in some form which makes it accessible to others is overwhelmingly difficult. Second, our personal knowledge is ephemeral and transient – it changes by the minute. Even if I were able to trap all my knowledge as of last week, by today it will have changed. How on earth could I possibly keep my knowledge archive up-to-date? Third, supposing that I had been able to trap all my knowledge for the benefit of others, how could anyone else find what they are looking for? Information stored for its own sake has no value at all: stored information has value only in so far as the appropriate information can be retrieved in response to a particular enquiry. This, of course involves catalogues, filing systems, key words and indexing – mechanisms of information retrieval which all depend on some advance awareness of how information, once stored, might usefully be retrieved. This book, for example, might be closeted away in some library somewhere under a heading such as 'innovation', and so can be retrieved in response to an enquiry such as 'Do you have any books on innovation?'. But if this is the only way in which the book is catalogued, then anyone asking the question 'Do you have any books on systems thinking?' or even 'Do you have any books which discuss the problems of capturing, storing and retrieving soft knowledge?' will not be directed to it.

If, as in many organizations, the barrier of an unwillingness to share information is high, then the barrier of just how to do it is overwhelming. So, needless to say, most organizations don't even try. Yes, they will introduce procedures for the capture and storage of hard information, and some organizations are more effective than others at making that work. Conceptually, managing hard information is not difficult; operationally, it requires well disciplined procedures; overall, the problem can be managed. Soft knowledge, however, is left well alone.

BUT WHAT ABOUT DATABASES, GROUPWARE AND THE INTERNET?

Until the last five or six years, the matter rested there. Recently, however, the technology of databases, groupware and the facilities of the Internet have dangled the lure that now, at last, the problem of capturing, storing and retrieving soft knowledge has been solved. Given the power of today's computers, the sizes of the databases that can now be built and the speed at which software products can scan literally millions of words, then problems such as the vast extent of personal knowledge and the difficulty of anticipating the nature of usage with the consequent need to second-guess the index, seem to have disappeared.

There is no doubt that, from a technical point of view, problems of size, speed and the logic of retrieval are at least receding, even if they haven't gone away altogether. But solving the technical problems is, to my mind, only part of the problem – and a small part at that. To me, the biggest problem by far is the capture of the knowledge in the first place. Before the database can be used by others, it must be populated, and the source of the contents of the database is you and me. How am I going to enter all my knowledge into the database? And how am I going to keep it up-to-date? First, I have to want to, with all the barriers of the '*Cogito, ergo sum*' mentality to be overcome; but second, I actually have to do it – I have to sit there and key in all that information. Who, other than the most dedicated computer freak, has the motivation, let alone the time, actually to do it?

IS THERE ANOTHER WAY?

Certainly, computer technology, databases and easy-to-use retrieval software provide a very powerful technical foundation for the building of an organizational brain bank. But the idea of a brain bank as being the collective archive of organizational knowledge is, I believe, not only impractical but also unmanageable. More importantly, however, I believe the idea of compiling the ultimate database of organizational knowledge is fundamentally flawed, in that there is a simpler approach – an approach that is much more practical, much more manageable and much more in sympathy with the human condition.

INDICES, NOT CONTENTS

The knowledge I carry in my brain is of two types. First, there is the detailed content – all the specific items such as those related in this book. But at a higher level there is an index: because I have particular interests, I know about, for example, innovation, systems thinking, the securities industry and so on. Within any one index heading, such as 'innovation', there is a wealth of detail which is vast, complex, ever-changing and ephemeral. But the index heading itself, 'innovation', is small (just a single word) and is simple, static and constant.

So, rather than creating a database of what I know, isn't it far easier to create a database of what I know *about*? This would be a database not of my brain content, but of my brain index. On an organizational level, such a database would not be very large and would be much easier to maintain, for any individual's brain index is much more stable than the underlying content.

AND THERE'S A ROLE FOR HUMANS TOO

But how would such a database be maintained? There will certainly be some individuals who are motivated to keep their own entries up-to-date but, in my experience, not many of them. So how might it be done?

By humans. By people who are motivated to maintain such a brain bank. By people who are computer-literate, and intrinsically interested in information storage and retrieval. By the sort of people who, today, are librarians or information officers.

Suppose, for example, that a particular information officer was assigned to you as your 'brain bank manager'. Every so often, the information officer would come to speak to you, to find out more about what you are doing and what you know. During this conversation, the information officer would use his or her skill either to compile your brain index or determine how it might have changed since the last time you both met. After the meeting, the information officer updates, as appropriate, the organizational brain bank not with the details of what you know, but with succinct information on what you know *about*. A large organization might have many information officers, all networked together through the computer databases which they collectively maintain. The databases themselves would make very good use of tools such as groupware, the Internet and any new technology which emerges and will probably have been designed by the team of information officers, because the design of structures to permit the efficient capture, storage and retrieval of information would be part of their expertise. Information officers are well positioned to be brain bank designers.

How would such a brain bank work?

Suppose you are about to attend a meeting of an industry-wide working party on, say, the European single currency. You don't happen to know much about it, and you want a brief. You contact your information officer and ask the question. The information officer then gathers together the hard data component, such as internal reports, external studies, newspaper articles and the rest. But, in addition, he or she accesses the brain bank to find out who in the organization has knowledge on this topic. If appropriate, your information officer can contact the information officers associated with those listed as having the relevant knowledge to find out the names of the experts and their contact numbers. You can then contact them directly, face-to-face, by telephone, by E-mail, using Lotus Notes, over the Internet, or however, so that the expert's up-to-date, specific, detailed knowledge can be shared with you. This direct contact ensures that the knowledge you receive is immediately relevant to your needs and completely up-to-date. This is supremely more satisfactory than reading some detailed database printout, compiled from knowledge captured possibly ages ago and with no anticipation of your particular needs.

This approach to the capture and sharing of knowledge is, to my mind, feasible and pragmatic. It makes the best use of available technology, but it does not attempt to trap every last item of detail: if we can keep track of people's brain indices, then there is no need to trap the content. Use of the brain indices can, through the medium of the network of information officers, allow the person who needs information to be put in direct contact with the person who holds it. And, once that point-to-point contact has been made, the appropriate knowledge content can be shared.

This does, of course, assume that the person who holds the knowledge is available and accessible – an assumption that will of course be invalid after an individual has left the organization. I would argue, however, that once an individual leaves, their knowledge is no longer soft but has become hard – static and historical. Your organization may or may not have a way of trapping it, but that is a different issue. Knowledge that has left the organization is always a problem but one which must be consigned to the past. Far more important is the problem of how best to capture, store and retrieve the information that is still within the organization.

I acknowledge that, arguably, the role I have described for the information officer is unnecessary. Once the concept of the 'brain bank as the organization's collective brain index' has been established and the appropriate infrastructure has been built, then each individual can, in principle, interact with the system directly. Thus the role of the intermediary information officer seems to be superfluous.

In principle, it may be. But in practice, in most of the organizations I know, such a role is exactly what is required to make such a system work.

Most people I know are just too busy, too computer-illiterate or simply too idle to operate such a system themselves. But, by the same token, most people I know would be only too pleased to spend the occasional hour or so with an information officer who then relieves them of the burden of maintaining the brain bank and provides the added value of making the brain bank work for them whenever they need to use it.

Indeed, to me, the role of information officer is potentially one of profound importance. By acting as the organization's 'knowledge hub' he or she performs a truly central function and is quite likely to end up knowing more about the organization than anyone else!

You may also be thinking that what I have just described – a system for the capture, storage and retrieval of knowledge, based on a network of personal interactions – is exactly how your organization works now, or maybe used to work before they fired all the staff who had been there for longer than ten years. My suggestion simply makes this very familiar process systematic and deliberate, comprehensive and sustainable.

Cogito, ergo sumus

A brain bank, of course, can only work in an appropriate cultural context. If I refuse to share my knowledge now, I will not change simply because my organization has spent a fortune on groupware or has designed a more efficient way to effect knowledge transfer. As I have emphasized throughout this book, the most difficult barriers to break down are not the technical ones but the cultural ones. I have also stressed that true innovation is an essentially human, behavioural, interpersonal process: a process which is all about sharing ideas; about appreciating that ideas need to be disaggregated and reshaped before innovation can happen; about allowing sufficient time for ideas to emerge fully fledged; about realizing that the building blocks of our ideas are our mental models; about experiencing how mental models can be explored so powerfully using the techniques of systems thinking and system dynamics; about recognizing that innovation takes place far more effectively within high-performing teams than by lone individuals; about rejoicing in how high-performing teams demonstrate cohesive action on the basis of coherent knowledge.

But this can only take place if the organization encourages and rewards the active sharing of knowledge. Only in this way can the whole be greater than the sum of its parts. The key concept here, as we saw in Chapter 8, is connectedness – the links that bind the component parts together. And in human organizations, this connectedness manifests itself in terms of communication and the transfer of knowledge. So, if your organizational culture is characterized by the tag '*Cogito, ergo sum*' – 'I think, therefore I am' – then, to become truly innovative, you have a long, hard task ahead of you.

No. '*Cogito, ergo sum*' is not the motto of the organization which shares knowledge and innovates. The organization which shares knowledge, and which therefore can and does innovate, has the motto:

Cogito, ergo sumus.

I think, therefore we are.

AFTERWORD

So bye now, gentle reader,
  You've had something pretty neat:
First a formal introduction to a boogie-woogie beat.
If the rhythm really got you, I do hope you stomped your feet
As you clapped your hands and rocked from side to side within your
  seat.

You now know that innovation – how to foster ideas new –
Is important for ourselves and for our org'nizations too.
No, it isn't inspiration, lightning striking from the blue:
There is science, there is process, there is lots that you can do.

And, yes, the answer's simple: **don't** *hire Newton, Einstein, Planck*
Or a bunch of friendly gurus to create your own think tank.
For to do so will bring failure as you'll surely draw a blank:
You'll ignore your greatest asset – your collective staff brain bank.

But what about to benchmark, or to copy, cheat, or steal
Someone else's bright ideas to help you reinvent the wheel?
Yes, this can help, but merely playing catch-up's not ideal:
If you're to win, then surely you must innovate for real.

Now you know the answer's different, for to nurture innovation
You must search your mental bound'ries to provoke the liberation
Of the power of the people in the whole organization:
That means you, and me and us – we all have great imagination!

Fine words, for sure, and oh so true; no, there has been no trap:
You've learnt the tools, techniques, the process, methods and the map.
Oh yes, you can inject your job with flair, pizzazz and zap!
Farewell, for now it's up to you – I hope you liked my rap!!

That's that!

BIBLIOGRAPHY

There are very many books on innovation, creativity, systems thinking and related subjects. I list here some of those that I have found particularly informative.

The Act of Creation, by Arthur Koestler, published by Hutchinson & Co., London, 1964.
A book of genius in which polymath Koestler delves into the nature of creativity by exploring the bases of humour, art and science. Very many of the seminal ideas – for example, those concerning patterns and the need to unlearn – are discussed most lucidly.

Techniques of Structured Problem Solving, by Arthur Van Gundy, published by Van Nostrand Reinhold Company, New York, second edition, 1988.
A veritable treasure trove of over 100 tools and techniques!

A Whack on the Side of the Head, by Roger von Oech, published by Creative Think, Menlo Park, California, 1992.
A lively canter through a range of tools and techniques, accompanied by the wisdom of the *Creative Whack Pack*.

Creative Whack Pack, by Roger von Oech, published by Creative Think, Menlo Park, California, 1992.
A pack of 64 'playing cards', each bearing an insightful message concerning creativity and innovation. Also available in disc format for use on personal computers.

Serious Creativity, by Edward de Bono, published by HarperCollins, London, 1993.
A compendium of de Bono's work over the last 25 years.

The Mechanism of Mind, by Edward de Bono, published by Jonathan Cape, London, 1969.
One of de Bono's earlier works, in which he proposes many of his models for thinking.

Children Solve Problems, by Edward de Bono, published by Penguin Books, London, 1972.
A wonderful illustrated collection of how children aged between 5 and 14 solve problems such as 'How to stop a dog and a cat from fighting', 'How to weigh an elephant' and 'How to design a bicycle for postmen'. A powerful exposition of 'the learning trap'!

I Am Right – You Are Wrong, by Edward de Bono, published by Viking, London, 1990.
An impassioned plea for constructive and cooperative exploration and debate, rather than destructive and adversarial advocacy.

Letters to Thinkers, by Edward de Bono, published by George Harrap, London, 1987.
A series of thought-provoking essays.

Six Thinking Hats, by Edward de Bono, published by Viking, London, 1986.
An exposition of de Bono's process for evaluating ideas safely, using the metaphor of wearing coloured hats to legitimize the key roles.

Six Action Shoes, by Edward de Bono, published by HarperCollins Publishers, London, 1991.
An action-oriented extension of *Six Thinking Hats*.

Managing Innovation, edited by Jane Henry and David Walker, published by Sage Publications, London, 1991.
A collection of papers with particular emphasis on how innovation can be encouraged and managed within large organizations.

Industrial Dynamics, by Jay Forrester, published by the MIT Press, Cambridge, Massachusetts, 1961.
The seminal text on system dynamics and systems thinking, which still reads freshly today.

The Fifth Discipline, by Peter Senge, published by Doubleday, New York, 1990.
A persuasive and articulate exposition of the role of systems thinking in management, alongside the four other key disciplines of 'personal mastery', 'mental models', 'shared vision' and 'team learning'.

The Fifth Discipline Workbook, by Peter Senge, Charlotte Roberts, Richard Ross, Bryan Smith and Art Kleiner, published by Currency Doubleday, New York, 1994.
A companion to *The Fifth Discipline* packed full of examples, explanations, discussions and anecdotes.

The Limits to Growth, by Donella Meadows, Dennis Meadows, Jørgen Randers and William Behrens, published by Universe Books, New York, 1992.
One of the most powerful demonstrations of how systems thinking can tame complexity on a global scale.

Beyond the Limits, by Donella Meadows, Dennis Meadows and Jørgen Randers, published by Earthscan Publications Limited, London, 1992.
An update on *The Limits to Growth*.

Managing with Systems Thinking, by Michael Ballé, published by McGraw-Hill, London, 1993.
A highly readable introduction to systems thinking and its application to management.

Competing for the Future, by Gary Hamel and C.K. Prahalad, published by Harvard Business School Press, Boston, 1994.
A lively and compelling argument from two of today's business gurus that business strategy is all about defining new rules for the competitive game – a game in which innovation is key.

Rethinking the Future, edited by Rowan Gibson, published by Nicholas Brealey, London, 1997.
A collection of interviews with a galaxy of leading business thinkers, including Peter Senge, Gary Hamel, C.K. Prahalad, Charles Handy and Michael Porter.

The Organisation of Behaviour, by Donald Hebb, published by John Wiley, New York. 1949.
The earliest book in which the process of learning is described in terms of the self-organization of neurons.

At Home in the Universe, by Stuart Kaufmann, published by Viking, London, 1995.
An exposition of the idea that the principle of self-organization underlies all biological processes. The author is a professor at the Santa Fe Institute in New Mexico – an interdisciplinary think-tank at the forefront of research on complexity.

Frontiers of Complexity, by Peter Coveney and Roger Highfield, published by Ballantine Books, New York, 1995.
An up-to-date survey of complexity theory, including the current thinking on self-organizing systems and on relevant aspects of the structure of the brain.

The Making of Memory, by Stephen Rose, published by Transworld
Publishers, London, 1992.
A lucid description of Rose's theories of brain function and memory.

The Astonishing Hypothesis, by Francis Crick, published by Simon &
Schuster, London, 1994.
In 1962 Crick, James Watson and Maurice Wilkins shared the Nobel Prize
for the discovery of the structure of DNA; this book presents Crick's
views on his current research into the behaviour of the brain and the basis
of consciousness.

How Nature Works, by Per Bak, published by Oxford University Press,
Oxford, 1997.
A compelling analysis of complexity and self-organizing systems.

The Rules of the Game, by Andrew Gordon, published by John Murray,
London, 1996.
The source of the anecdotes about Nelson and the Battle of Jutland retold
in Chapter 13, and, although written as a history of the British Navy, it is
also a most stimulating book on management.

INDEX